Mel Bay Presents

SONGS & SOLOS FOR UKE

By Ken Eidson & Ross Cherednik

1 2 3 4 5 6 7 8 9 0

© 1984 BY MEL BAY PUBLICATIONS, INC. PACIFIC, MO.
INTERNATIONAL COPYRIGHT SECURED. ALL RIGHTS RESERVED. PRINTED IN U.S.A.

THE AUTHORS

Ken Eidson

Ross Cherednik

Ross Cherednik with Uke custom built by David Gomes.

TABLE OF CONTENTS

Crawdad Song	4
Rye Whiskey	6
Banks of the Ohio	8
The Roving Cowboy	10
Red Rocking Chair	12
Silent Night	14
Blow Away the Morning Dew	16
Greenland Fishery	18
Bury Me Out on the Lone Prairie	20
The Drunken Sailor	22
Knoxville Girl	24
The Blue-Tail Fly	26
The Girl I Left Behind	28
The Big Rock Candy Mountain	30
The Ash Grove	33
Home on the Range	36
Blow, Ye Winds	38
Sweet Betsy from Pike	40
Down in the Valley	42
Little Brown Jug	44
Oh Suzanna	46
Shenandoah	48
Turkey in the Straw	50
There is a Tavern in the Town	52
Rio Grande	56
John Hardy	58
Red River Valley	60
Yankee Doodle	62
Aloha Oe	64
Johnny Has Gone for a Soldier	66
Goober Peas	68
A-Roving	70
Chisholm Trail	72
Deep River	74
Basic Chords	76
Notes on the Fingerboard	77
Scales	78

For information concerning tapes of the songs
in this book, write to:
Ken Eidson, 2121 Linneman St., Glenview, Illinois 60025

CRAWDAD SONG

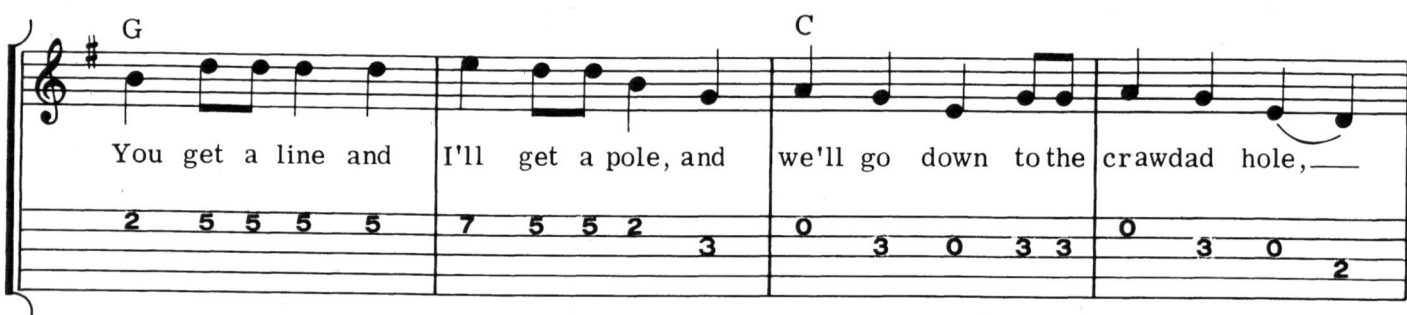
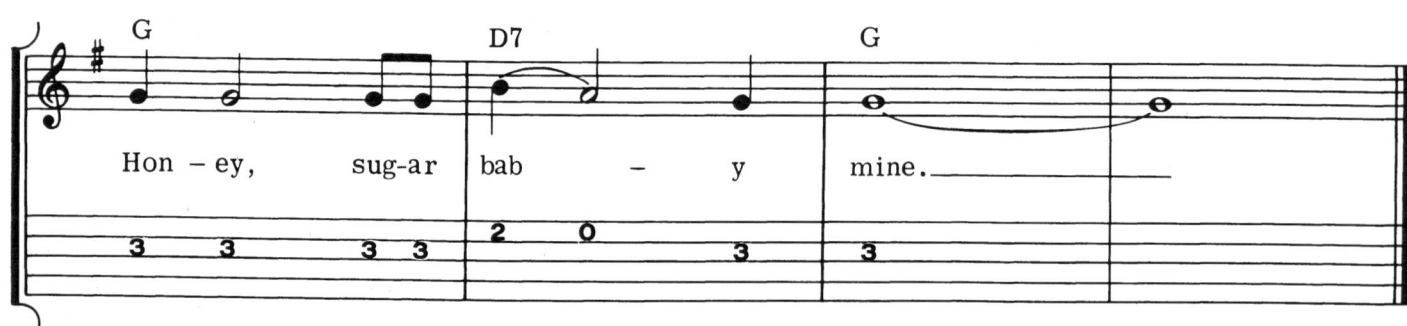

What you gonna do when the lake runs dry honey?
What you gonna do when the lake runs dry babe?
What you gonna do when the lake runs dry,
Sit on the bank and watch the crawdads die,
Honey, sugar baby mine.

CRAWDAD SONG

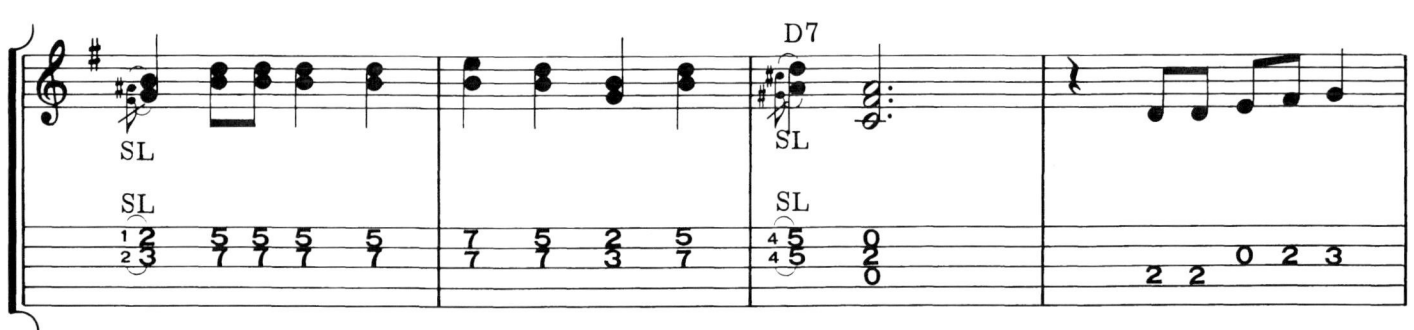
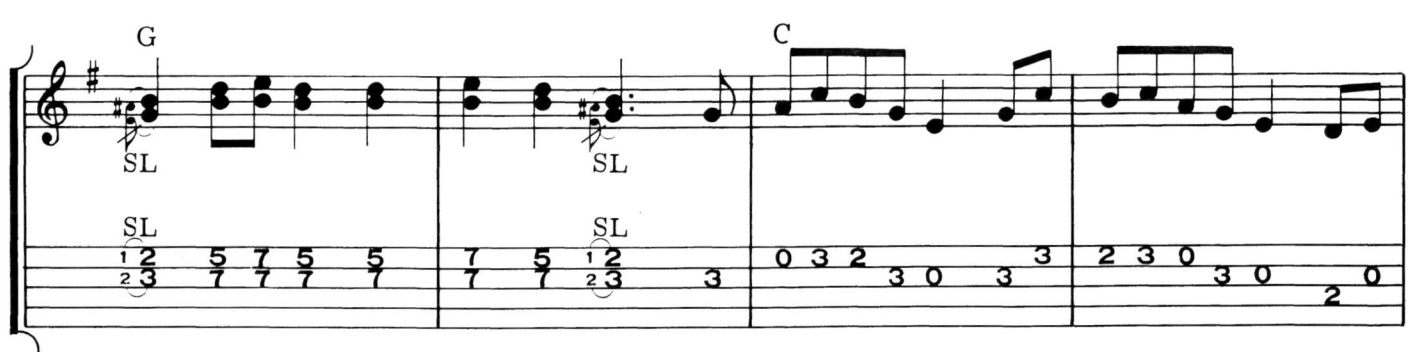

RYE WHISKEY

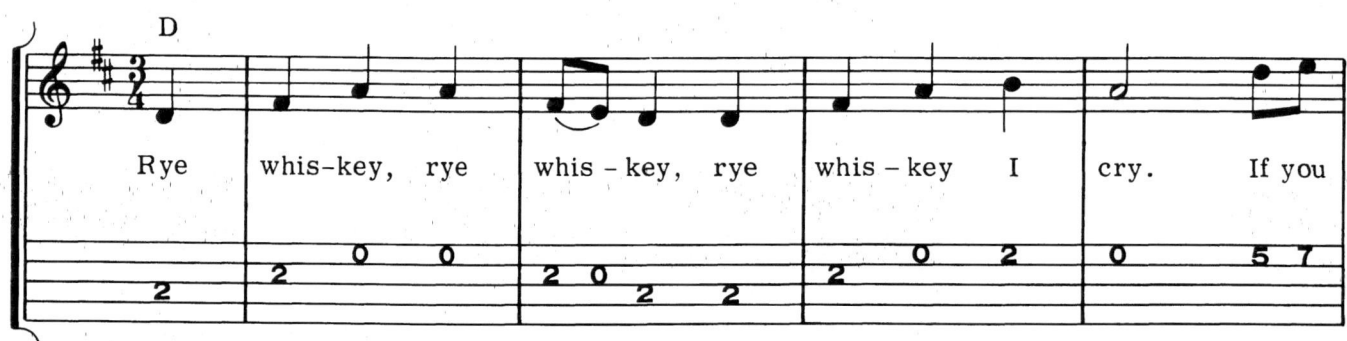
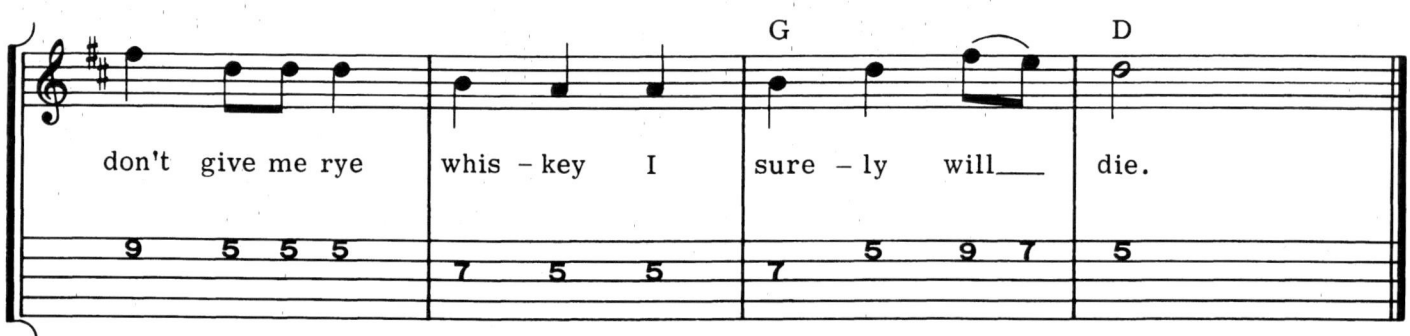

If the ocean was whiskey and I was a duck,
I'd dive to the bottom and never come up.

Way up on Clinch Mountain I wander alone.
I'm drunk as the devil, just leave me alone.

I eat when I'm hungry, I drink when I'm dry.
If a tree don't fall on me I'll live till I die.

RYE WHISKEY

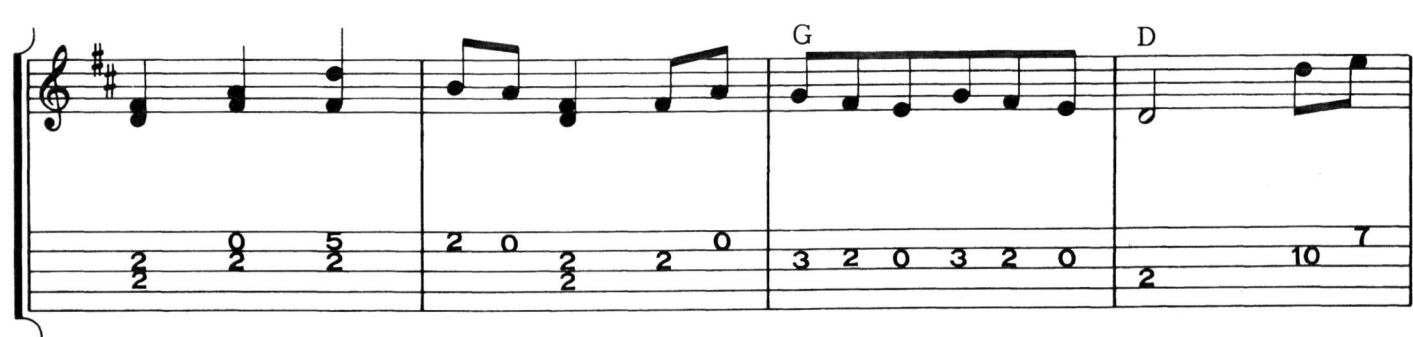
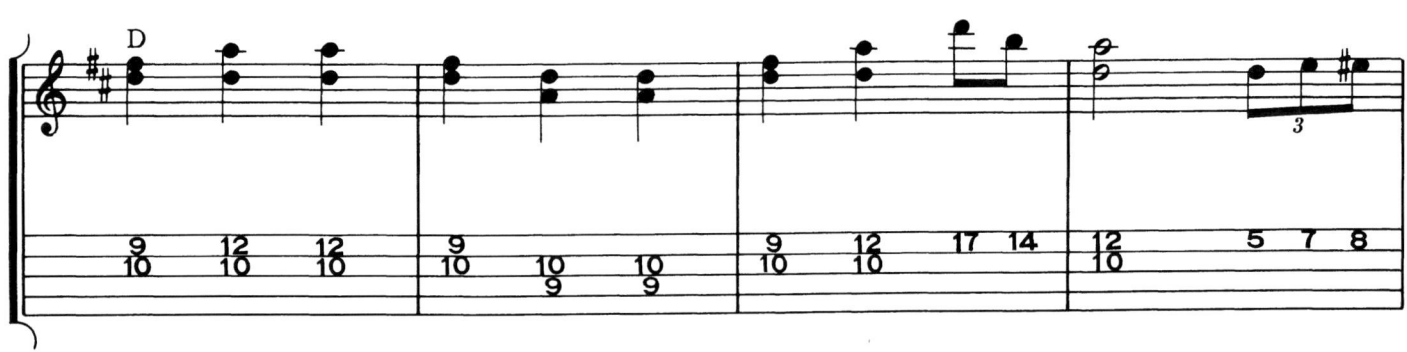

BANKS OF THE OHIO

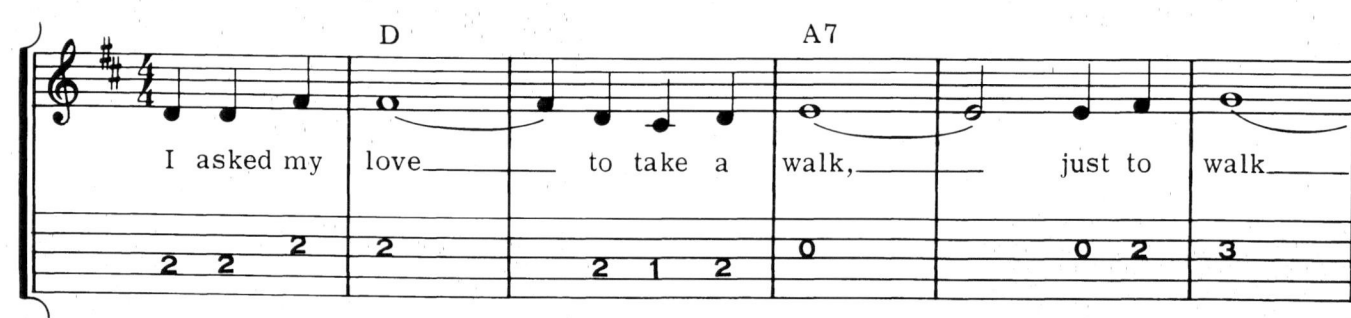
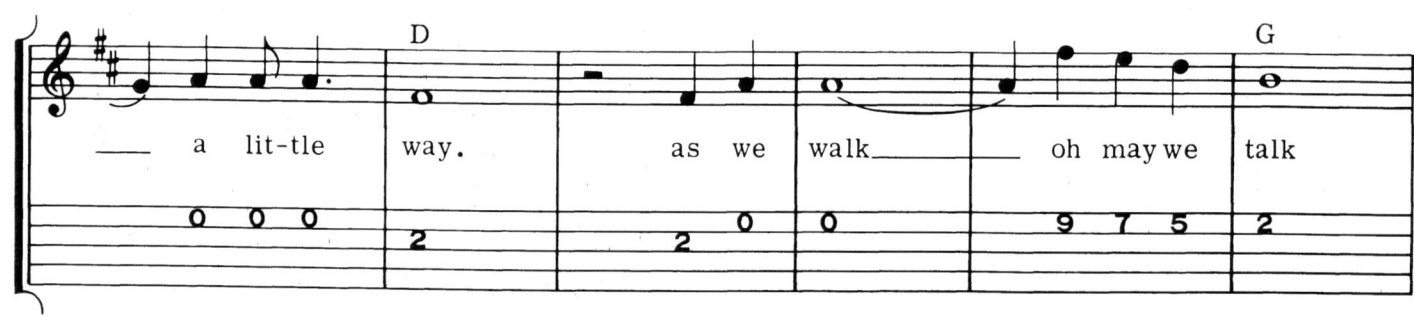
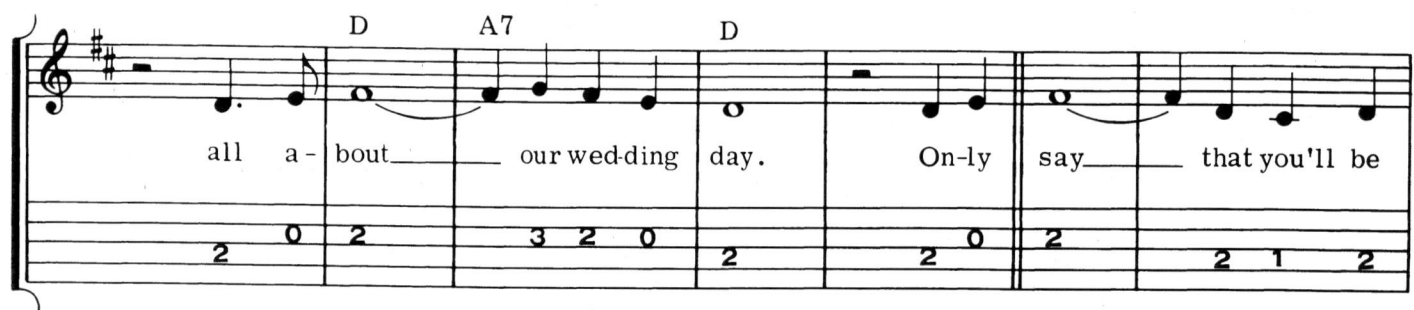

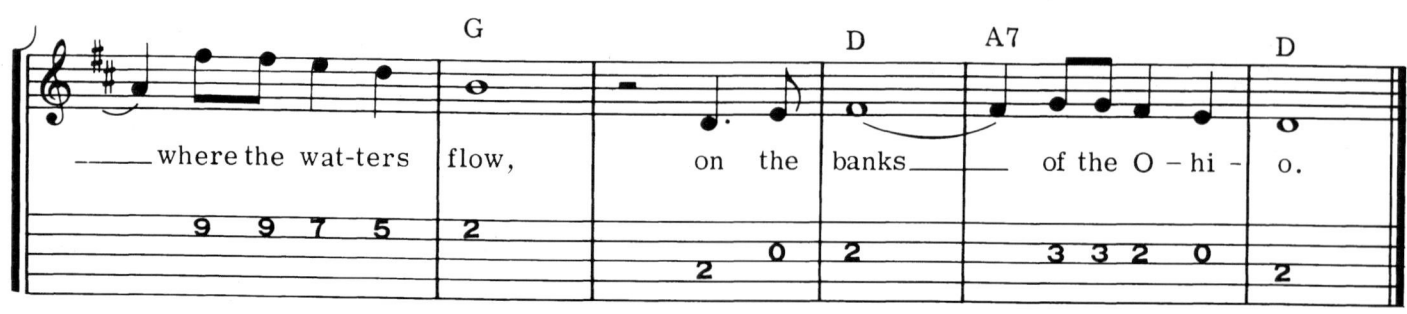

BANKS OF THE OHIO

THE ROVING COWBOY

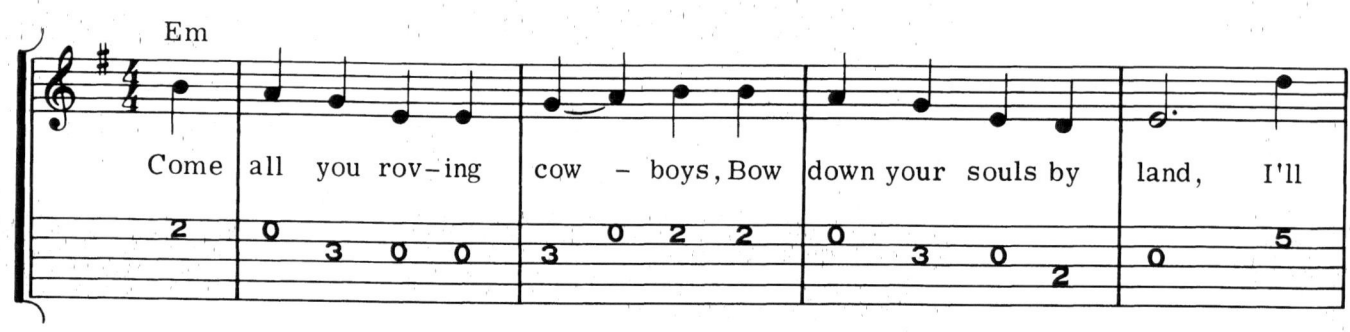
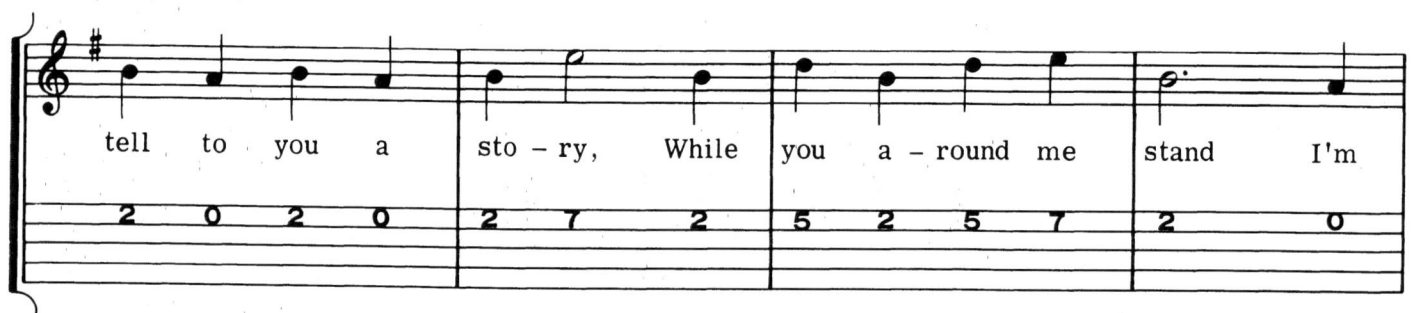
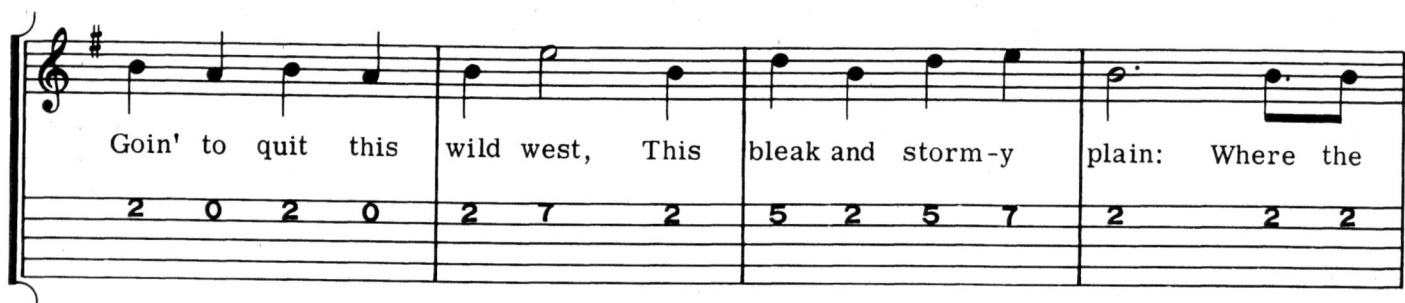
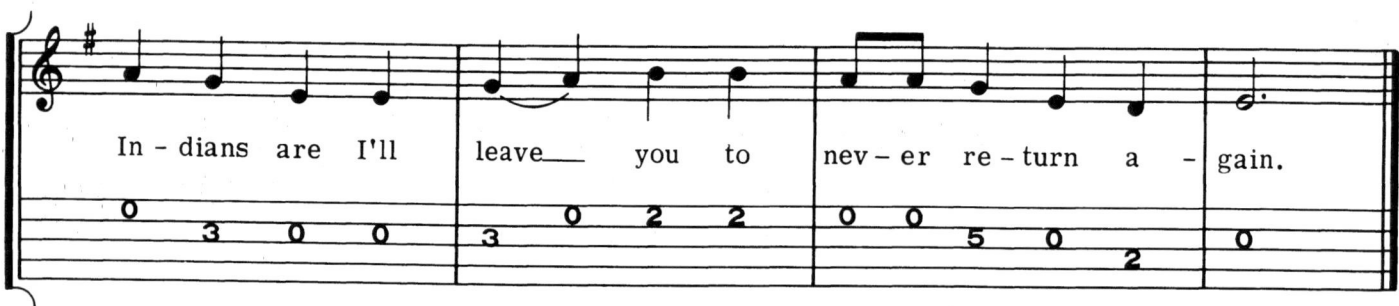

I've crossed the Rocky Mountains, I've crossed the Rocky Hills;
I've crossed the Rocky Mountains where many a brave boy's fell;
I've seen the distant country, the Indians and the Wild:
I'll never forget my old, old home, and mother's sweetest smile.

THE ROVING COWBOY

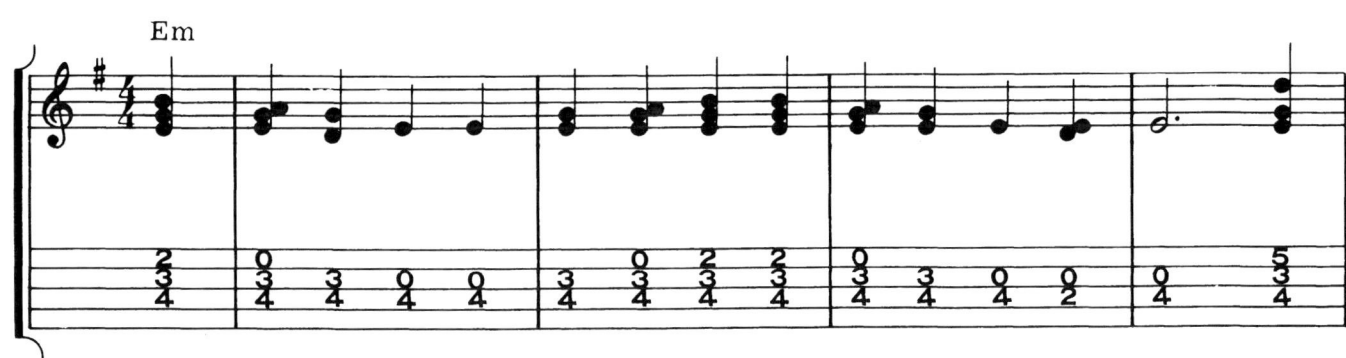
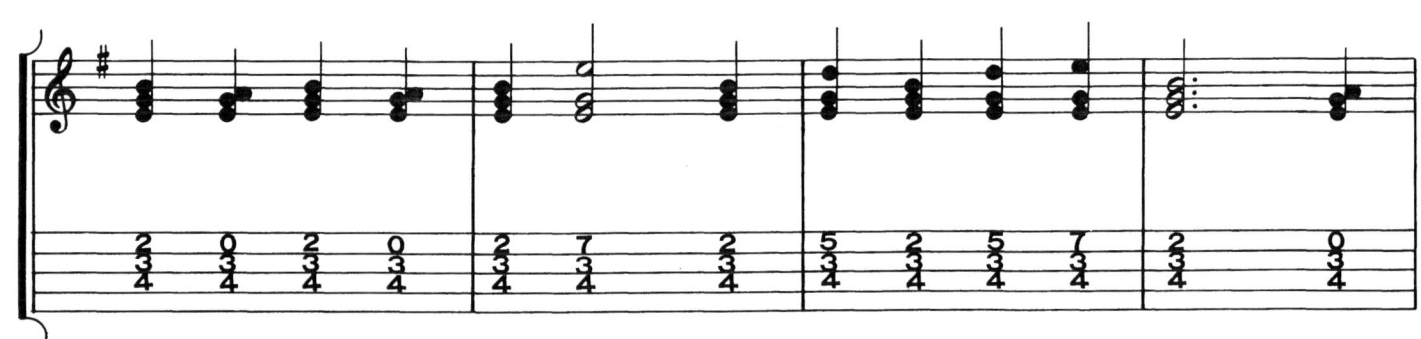
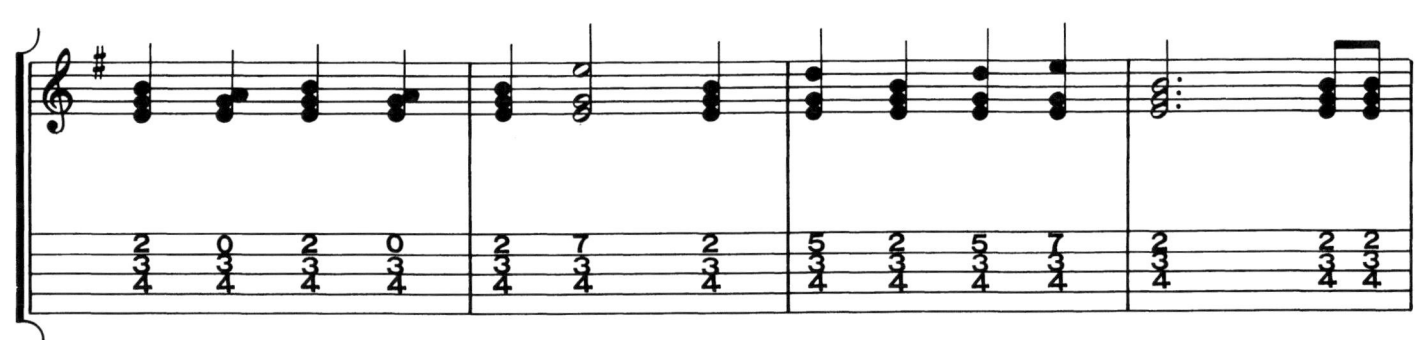
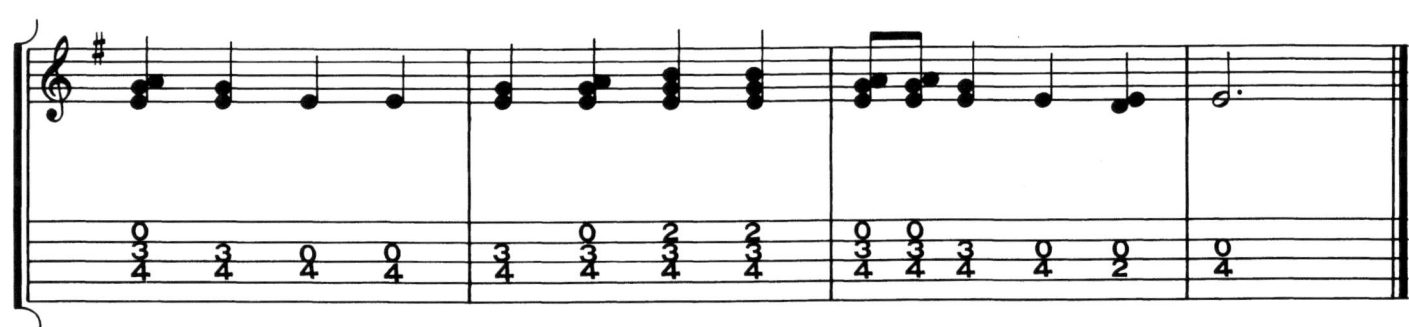

RED ROCKING CHAIR

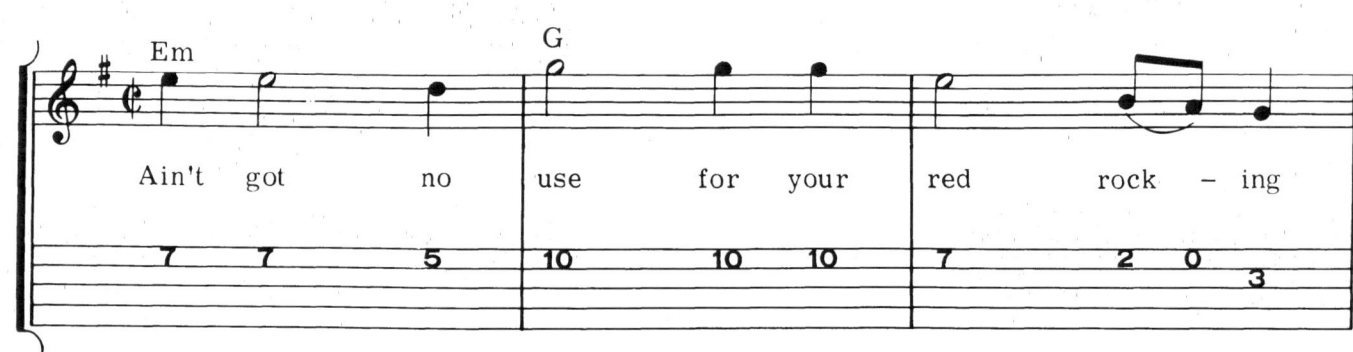

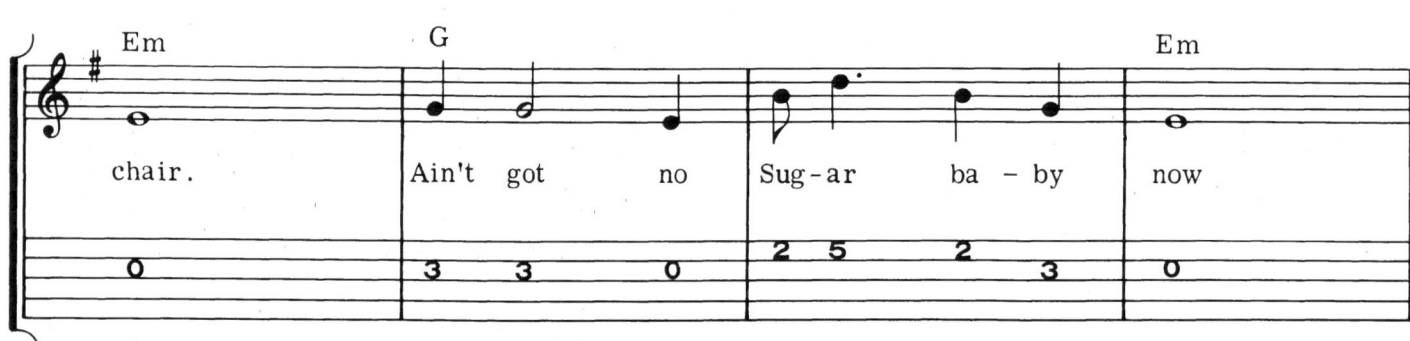

Who'll rock the cradle, who'll sing the song,
Who'll rock the cradle, when I'm gone,
It's who'll rock the cradle when I'm gone.

I'll rock the cradle, I'll sing the song,
I'll rock the cradle when you're gone,
It's I'll rock the cradle when you're gone.

It's all I can do, It's all I can say,
I can't get along this-a-way,
I can't get along this-a-way.

RED ROCKING CHAIR

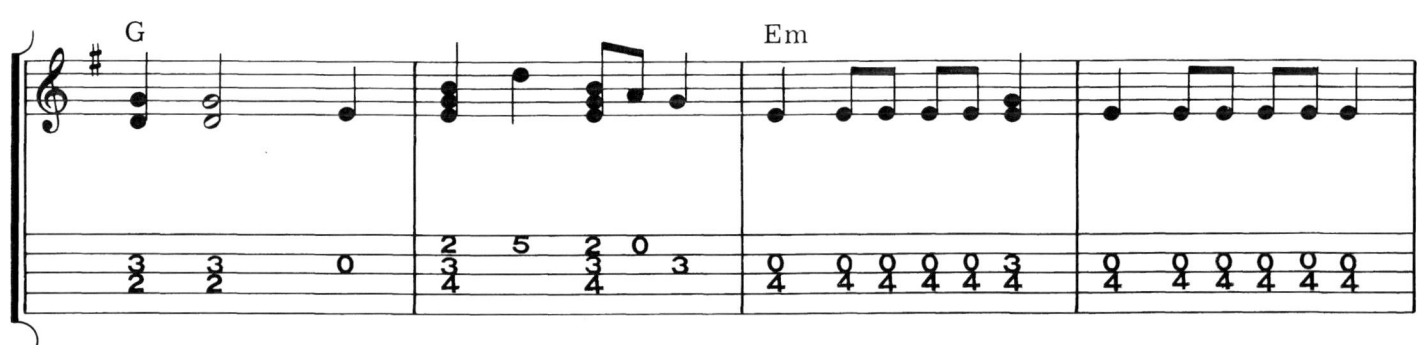

SILENT NIGHT

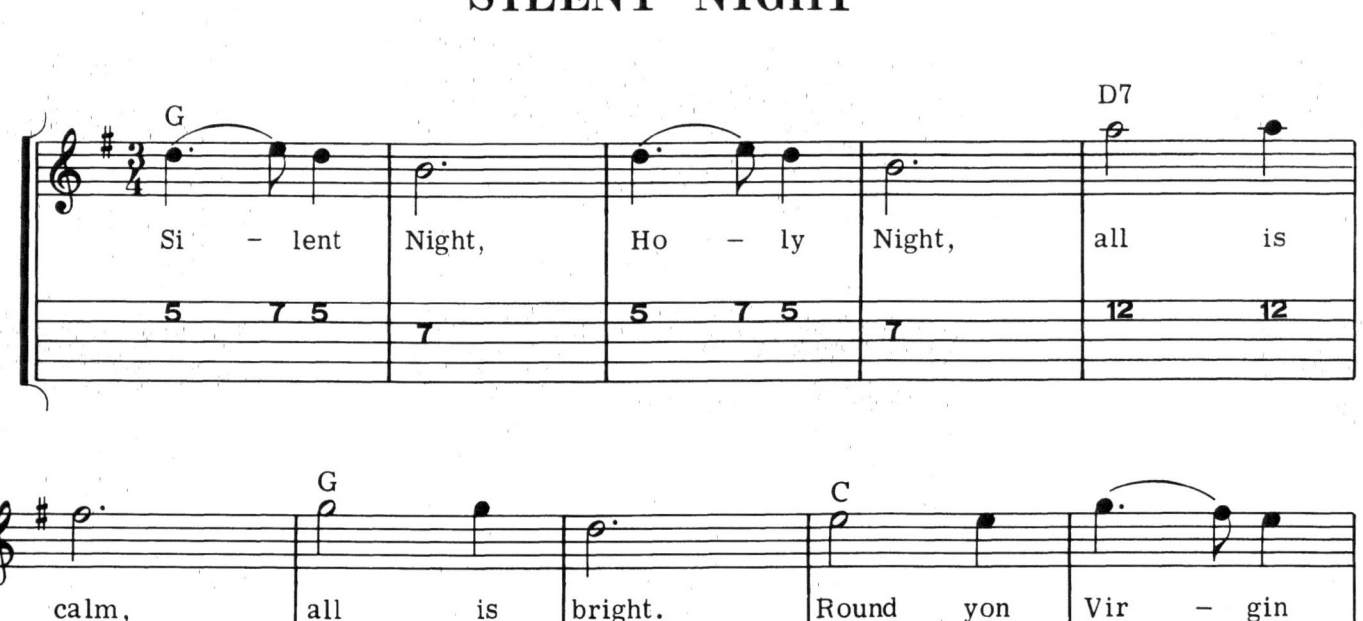
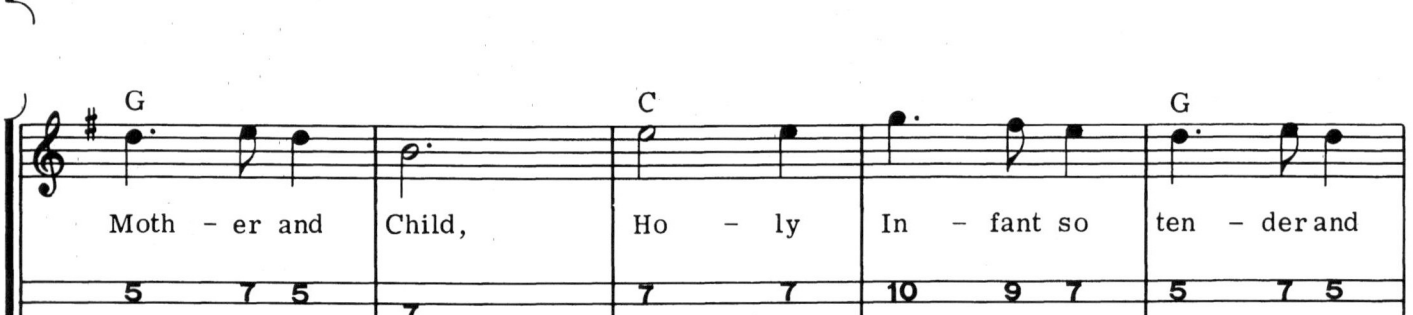
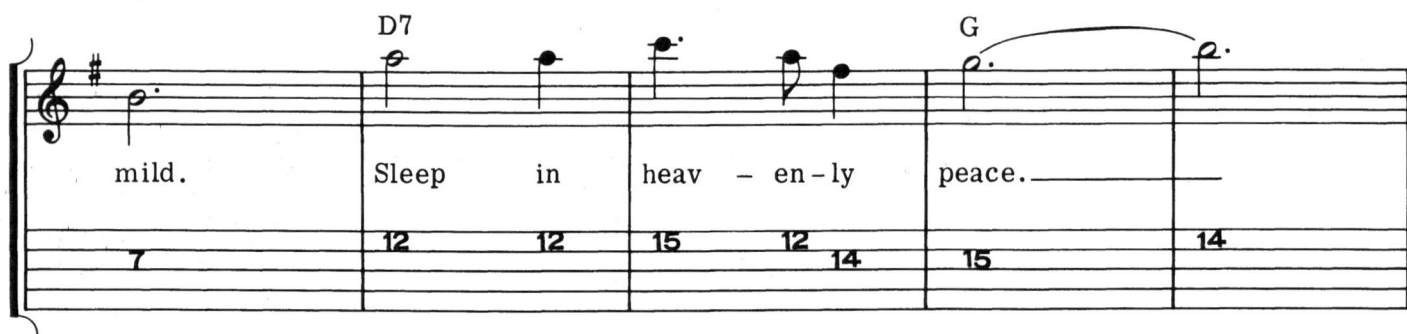
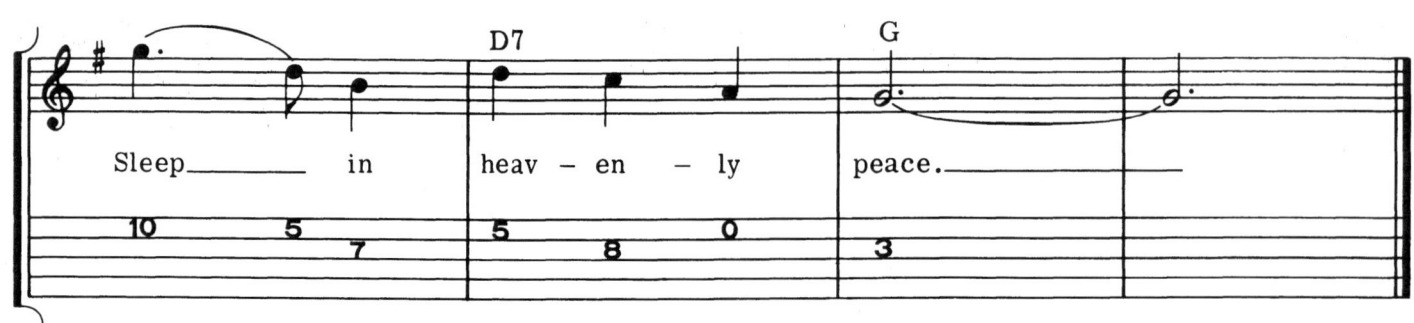

SILENT NIGHT

BLOW AWAY THE MORNING DEW

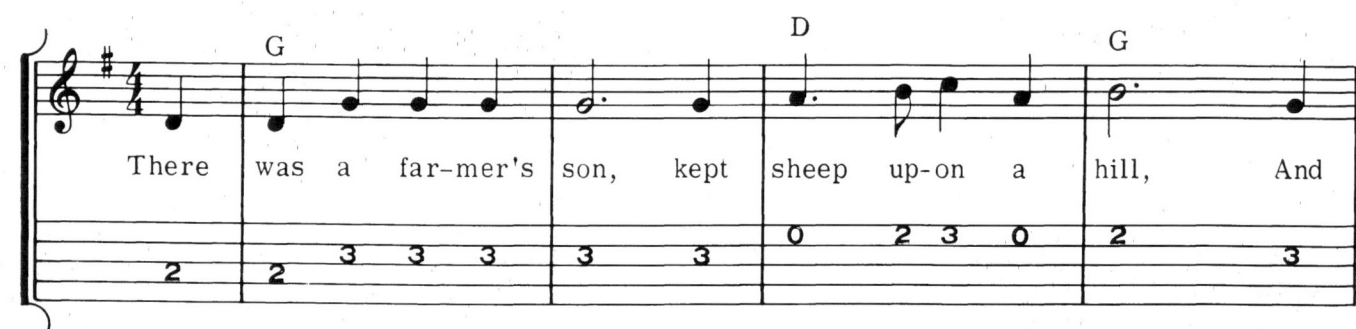
There was a farmer's son, kept sheep upon a hill, And

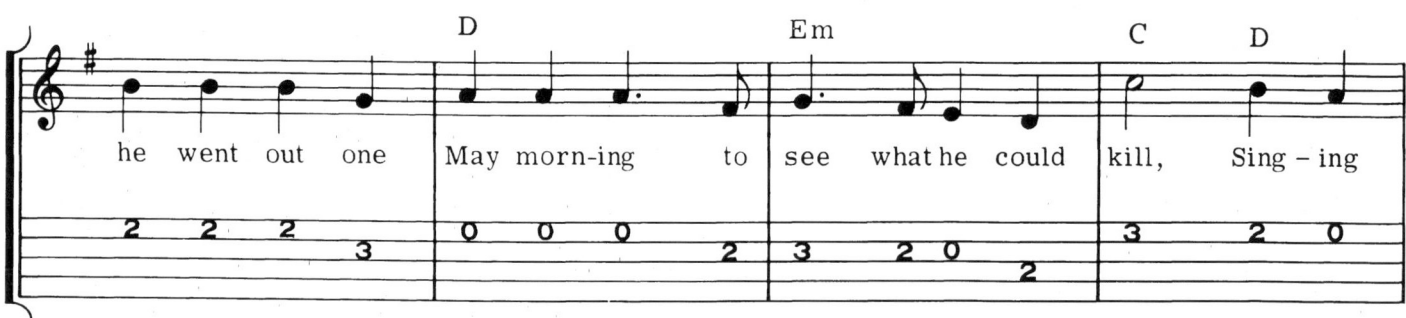
he went out one May morning to see what he could kill, Singing

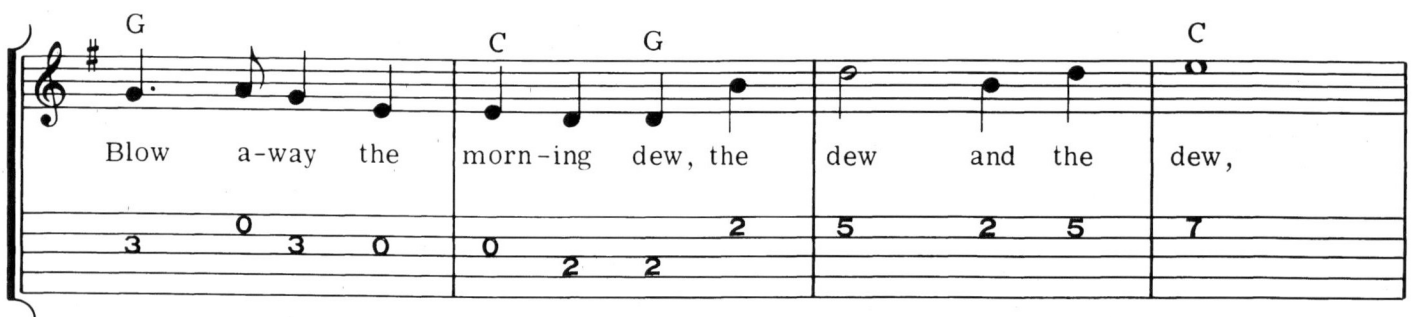
Blow away the morning dew, the dew and the dew,

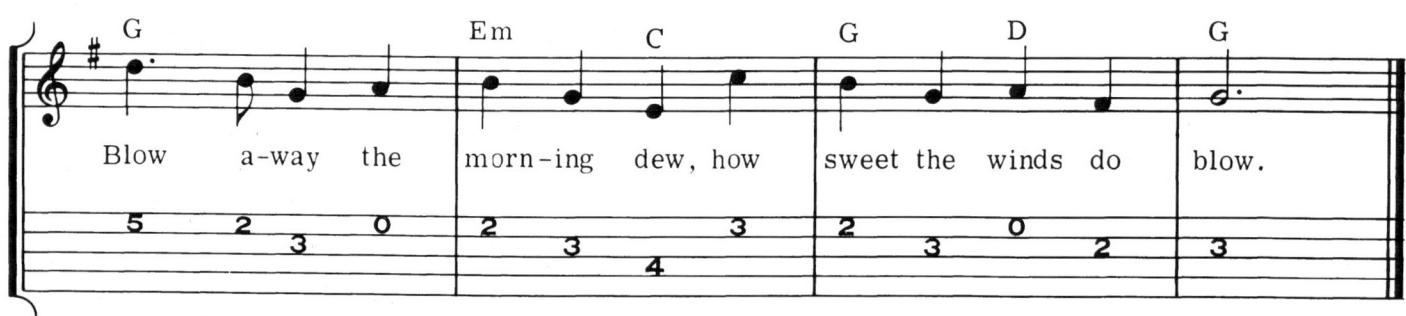
Blow away the morning dew, how sweet the winds do blow.

He looked high, he looked low, he cast an under look,
And there he saw a fair pretty maid, a-bathing in the brook,
Singing, Blow away the morning dew.................
If you will come to my father's house which is walled all around,
Then you shall have your will of me and twenty thousand pound,
Singing, Blow away the morning dew.................
But when they came to her father's gate, so quickly she popped in,
And said, "There stands a fool without, and here's a maid within"
Singing, Blow away the morning dew.................

BLOW AWAY THE MORNING DEW

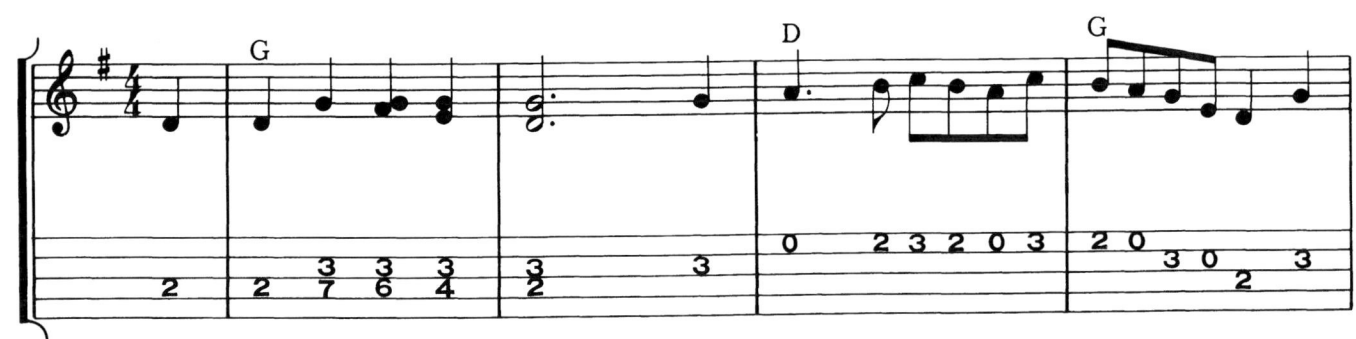
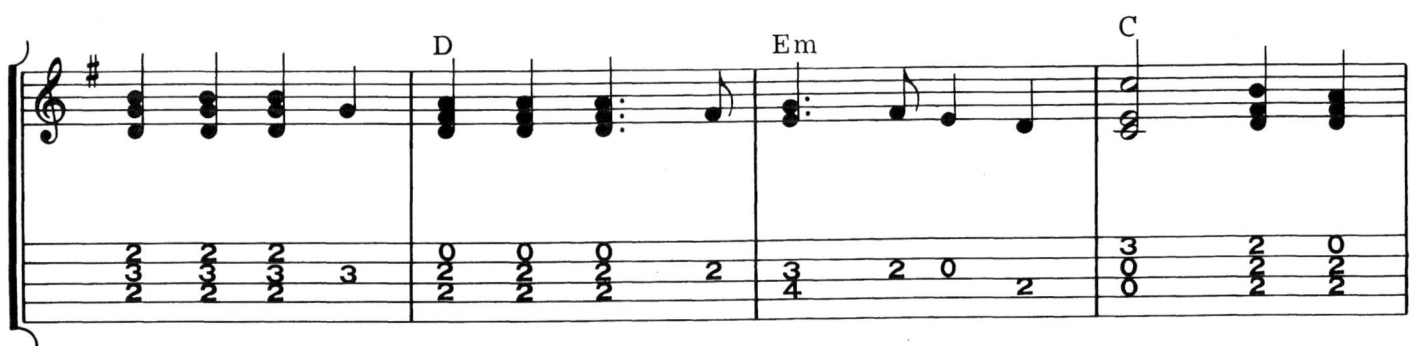

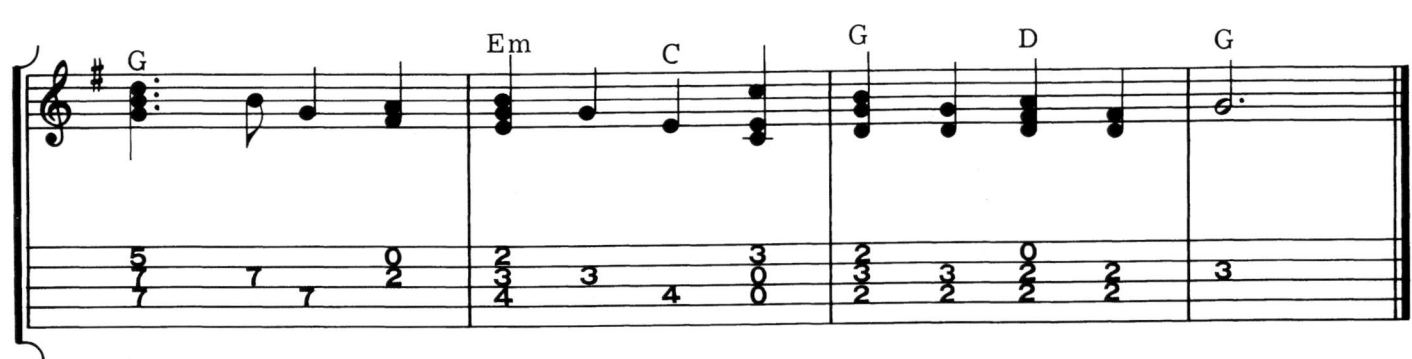

GREENLAND FISHERY

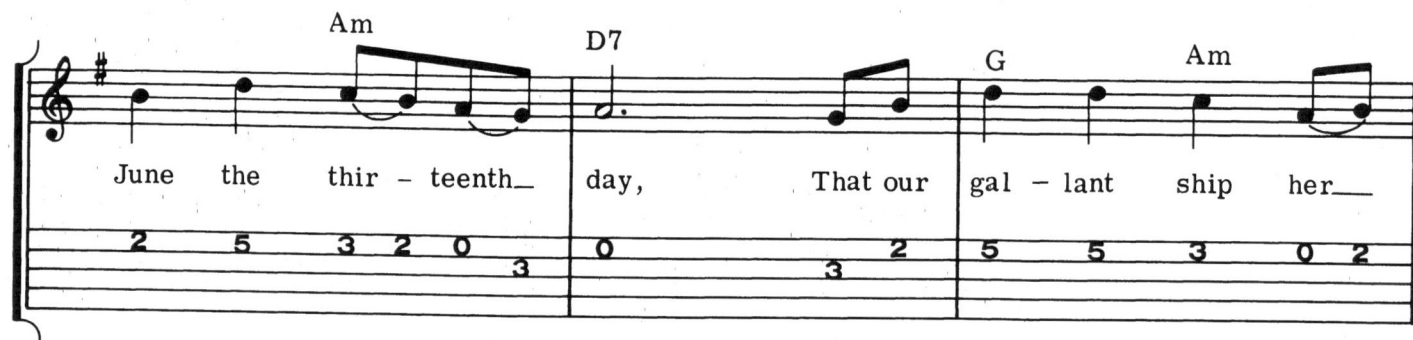
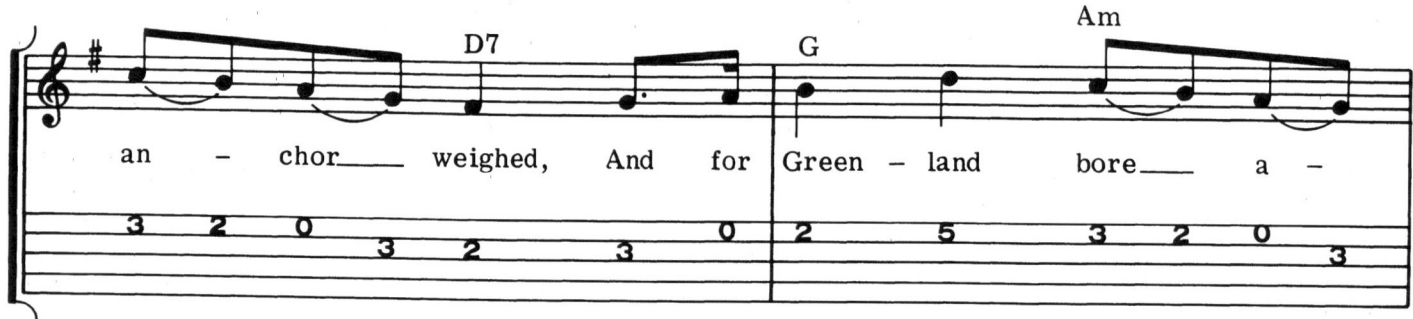
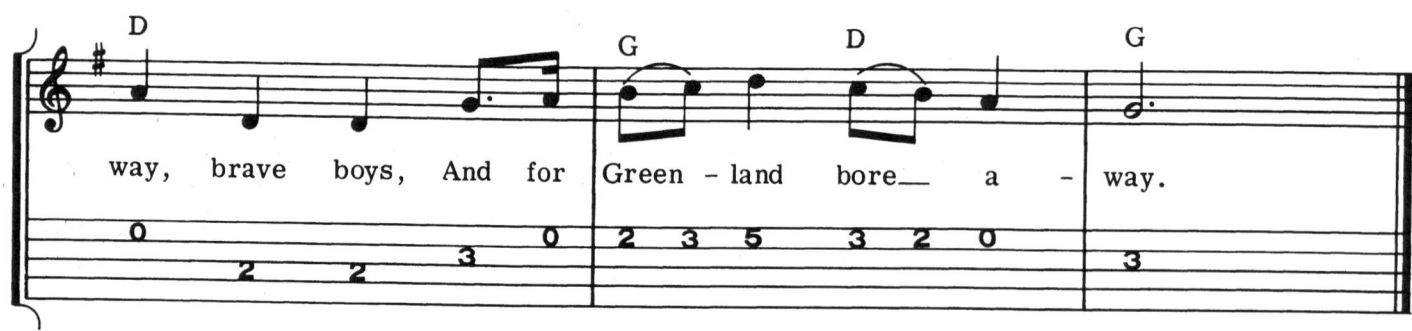

The lookout in the crosstrees stood,
With his spy glass in his hand.
"There's a whale, there's a whale, there's a whalefish," he cried,
"And she blows at every span, brave boys,
And she blows at every span."

GREENLAND FISHERY

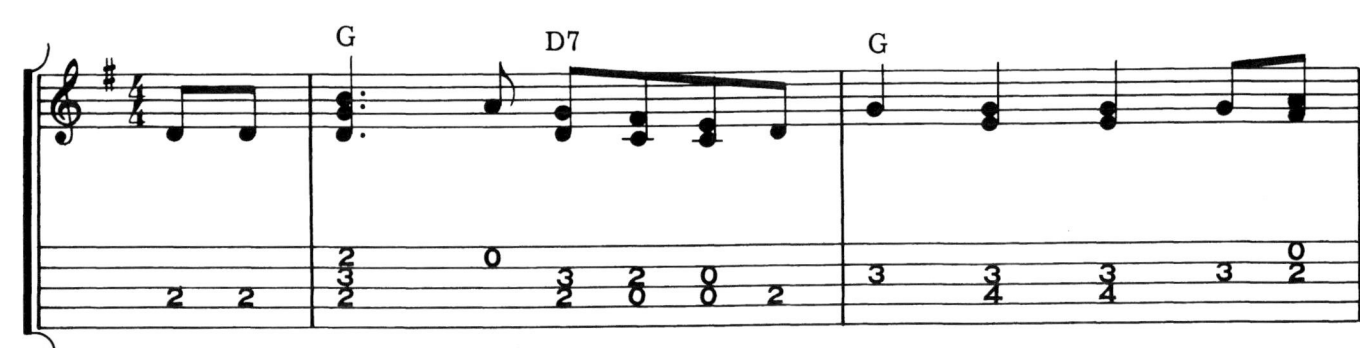
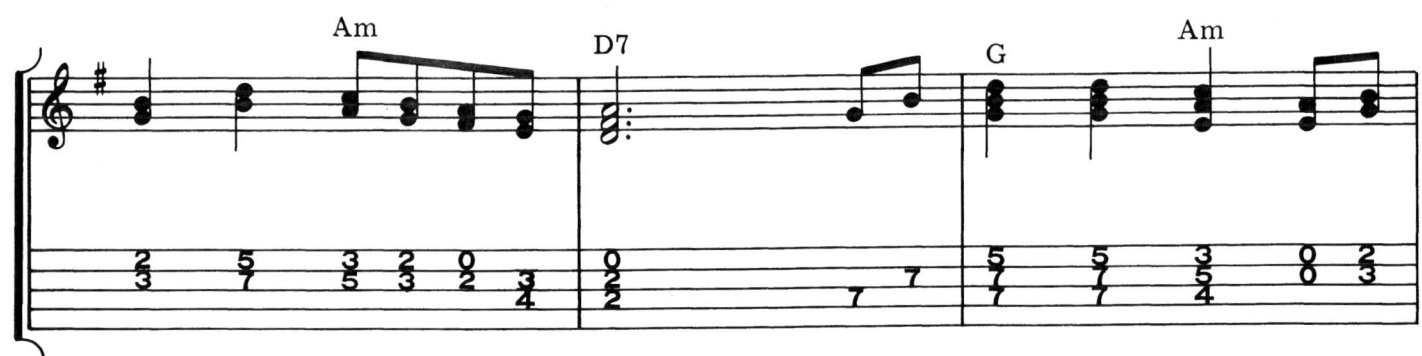
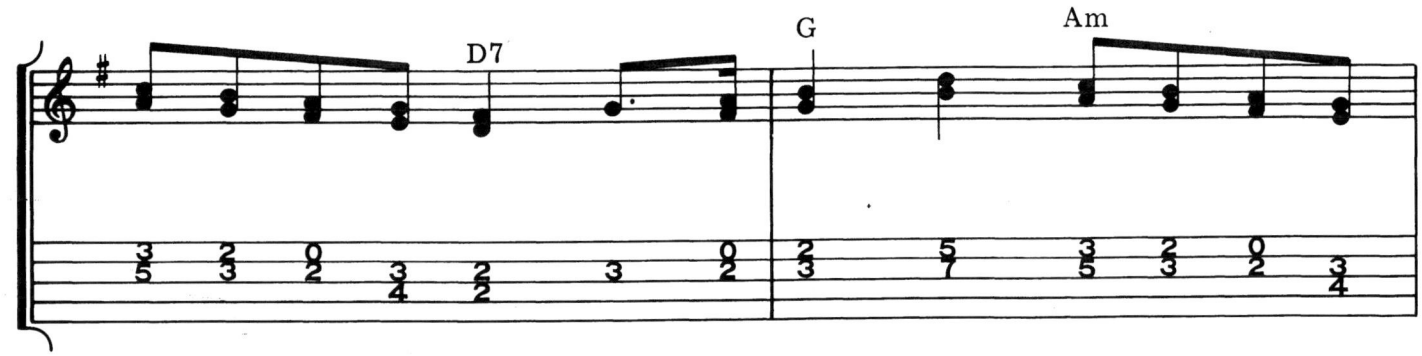
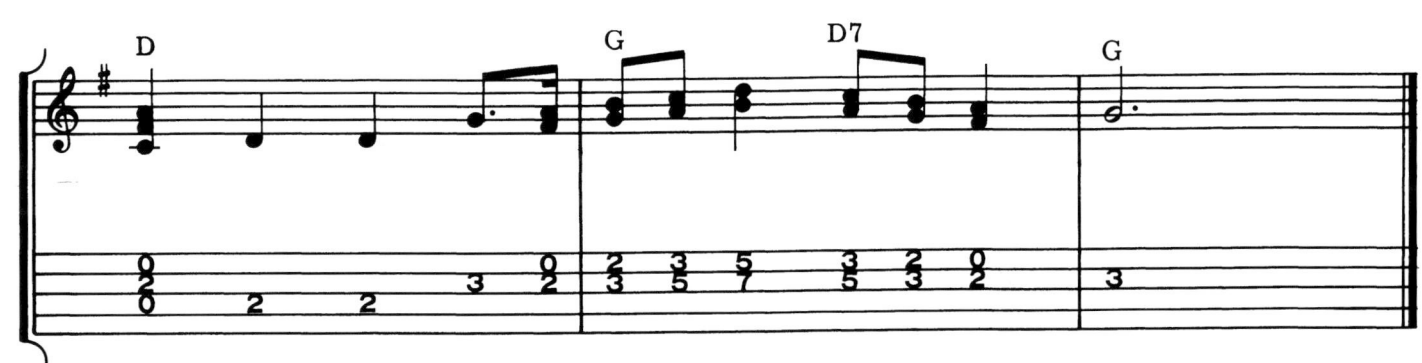

BURY ME OUT ON THE LONE PRAIRIE

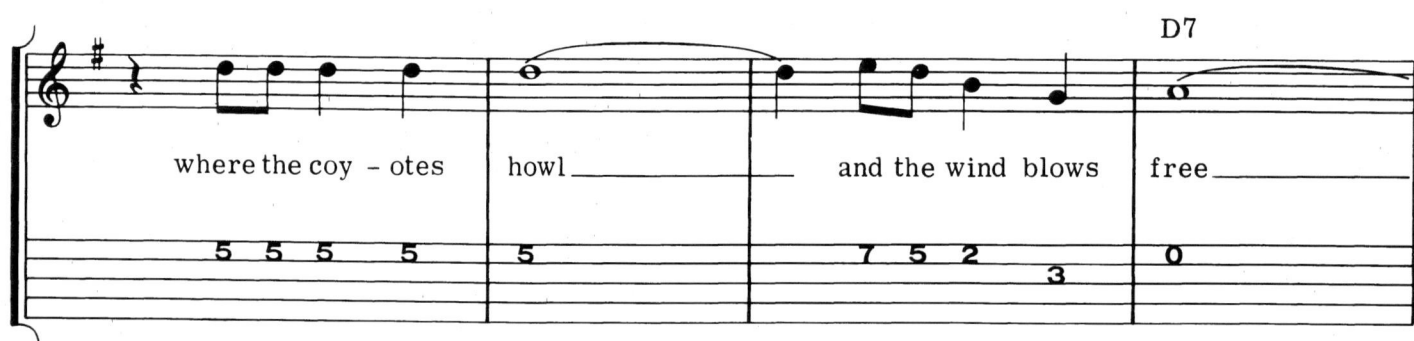

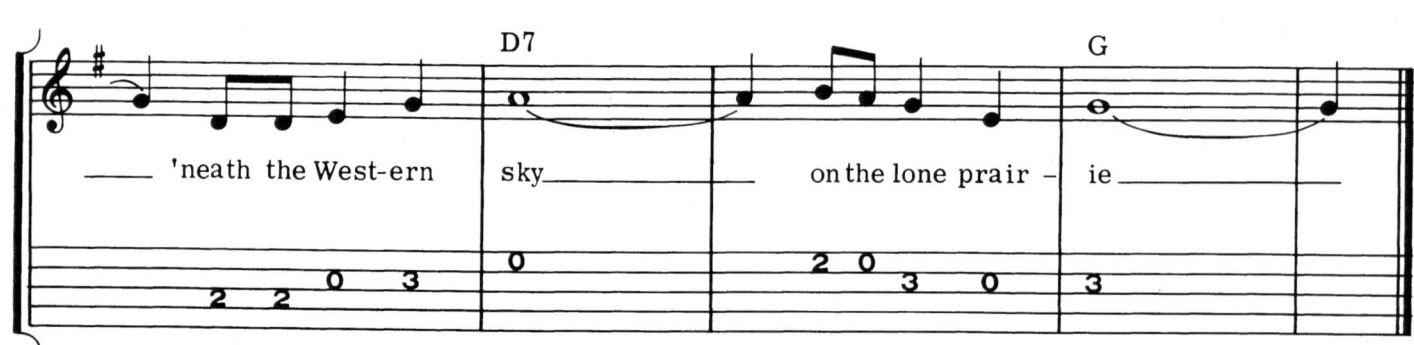

BURY ME OUT ON THE LONE PRAIRIE

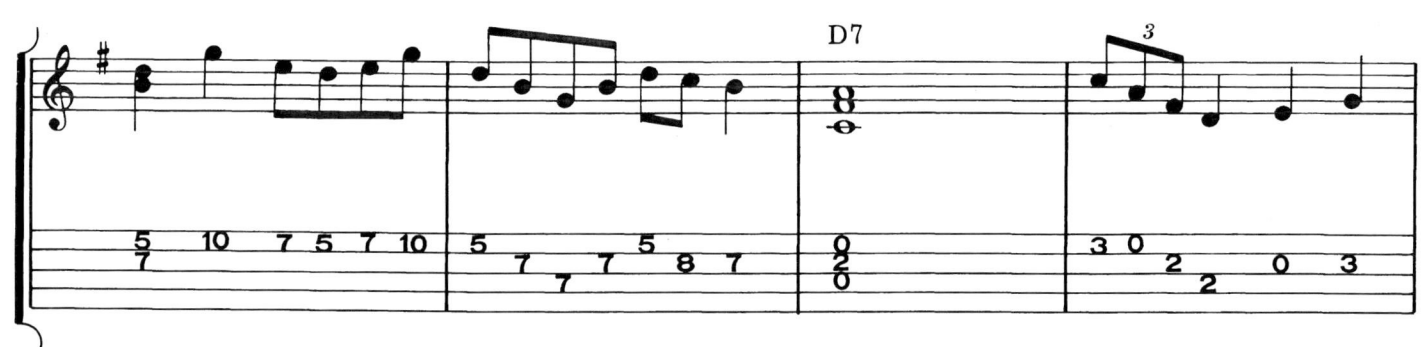
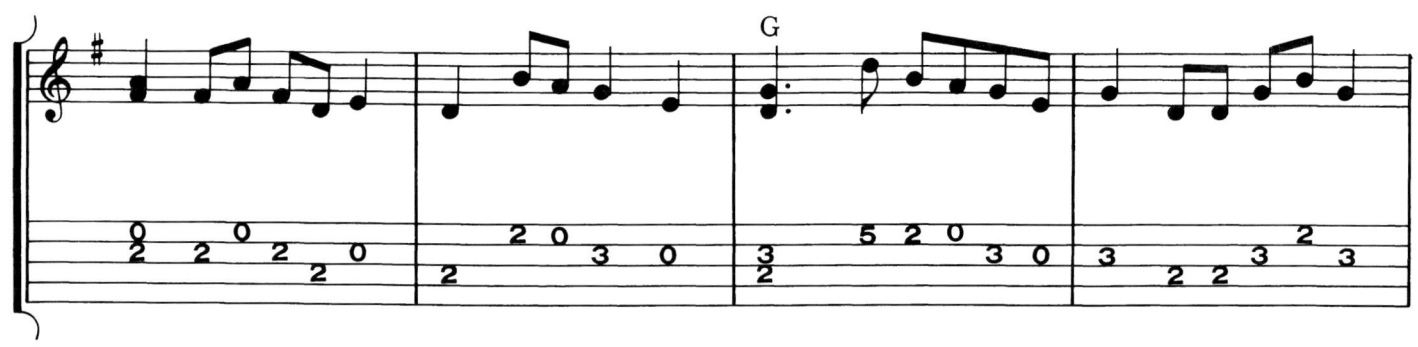

THE DRUNKEN SAILOR

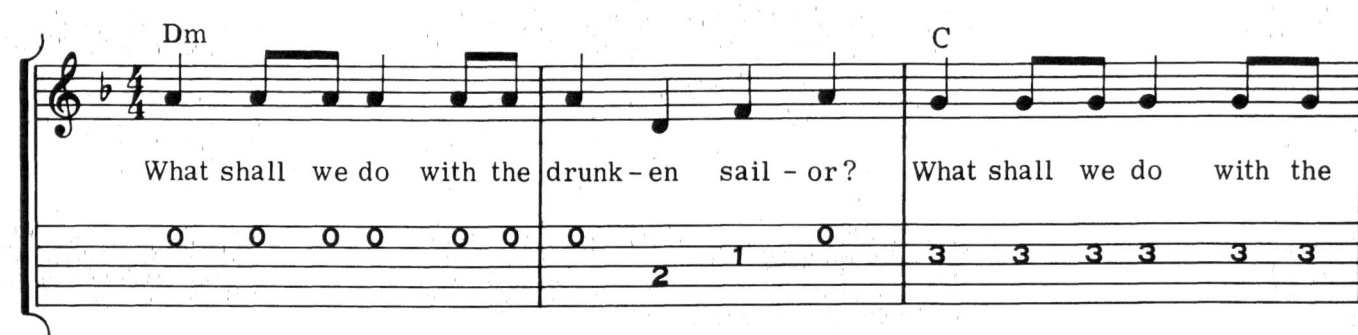
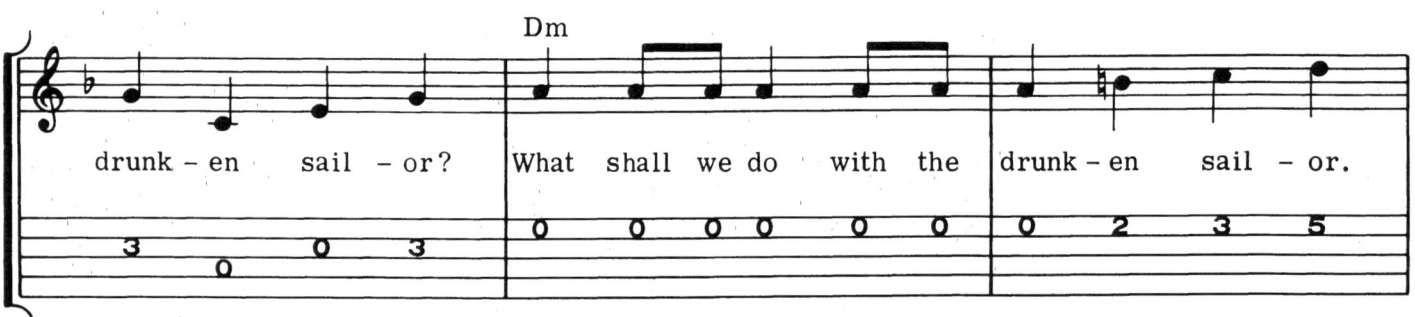
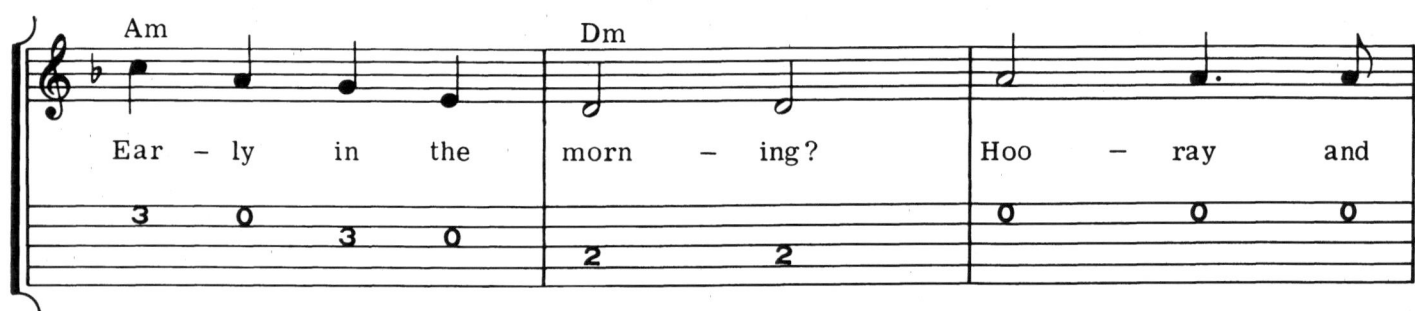

THE DRUNKEN SAILOR

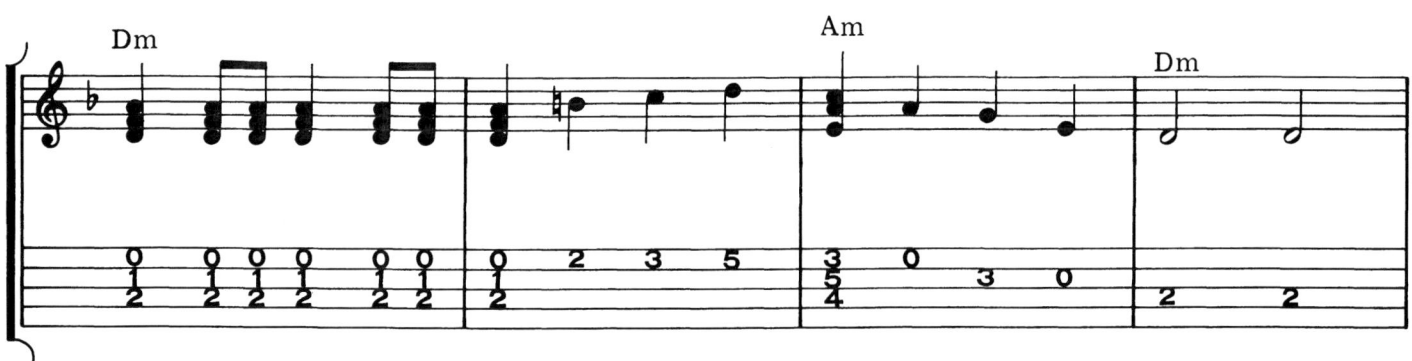
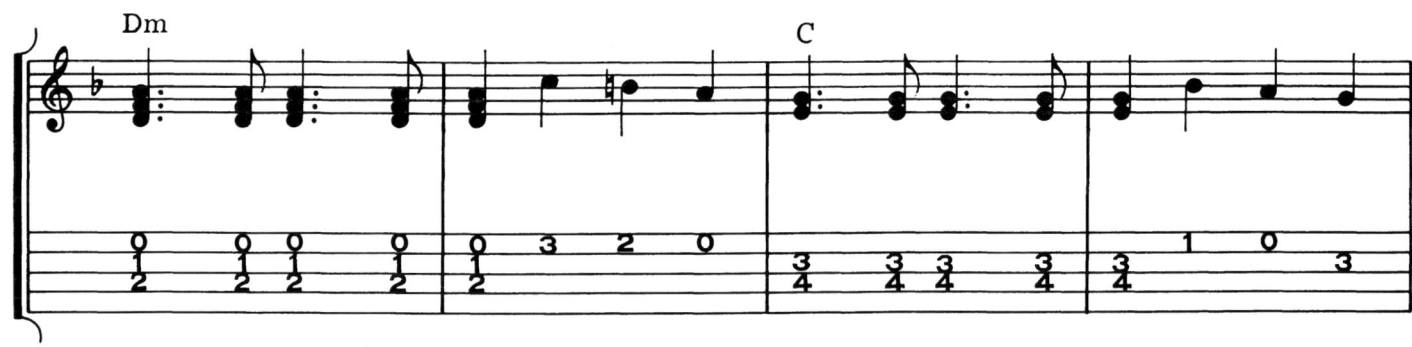
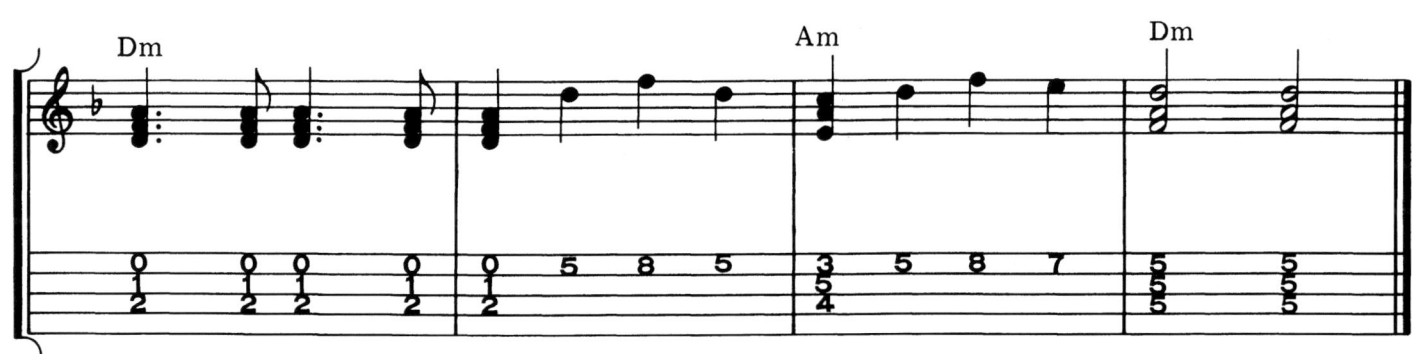

KNOXVILLE GIRL

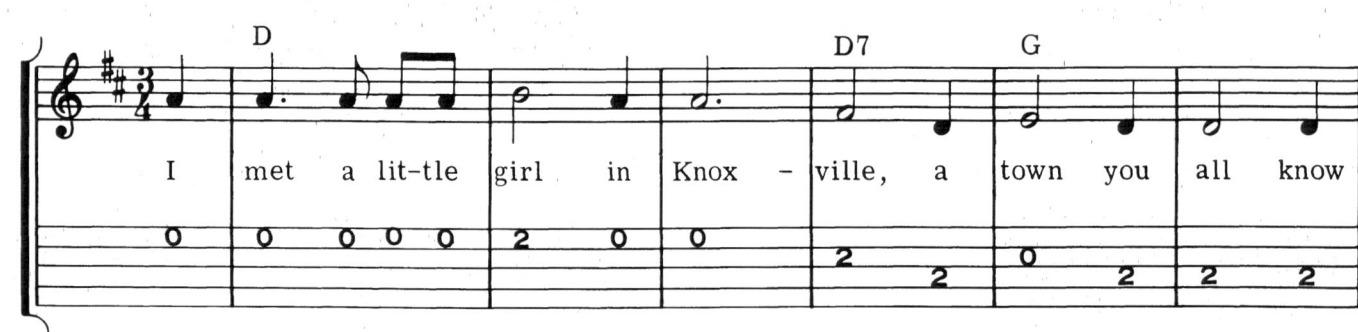
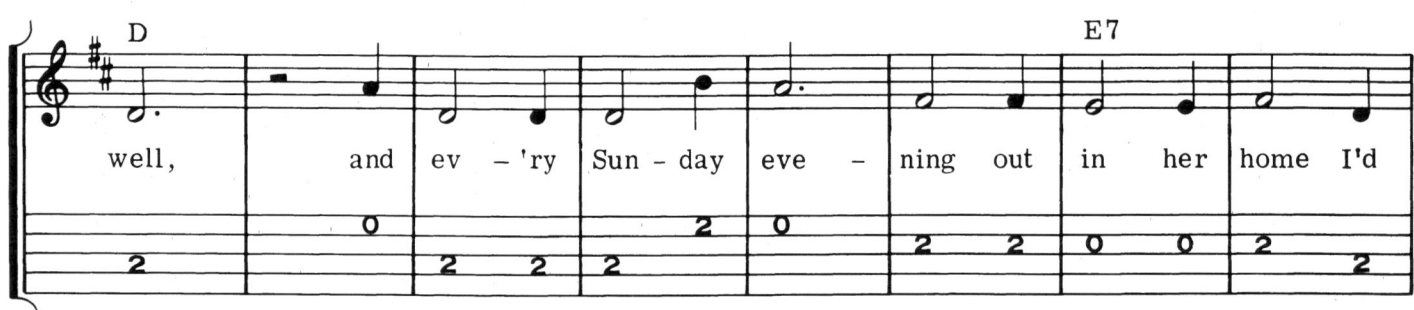
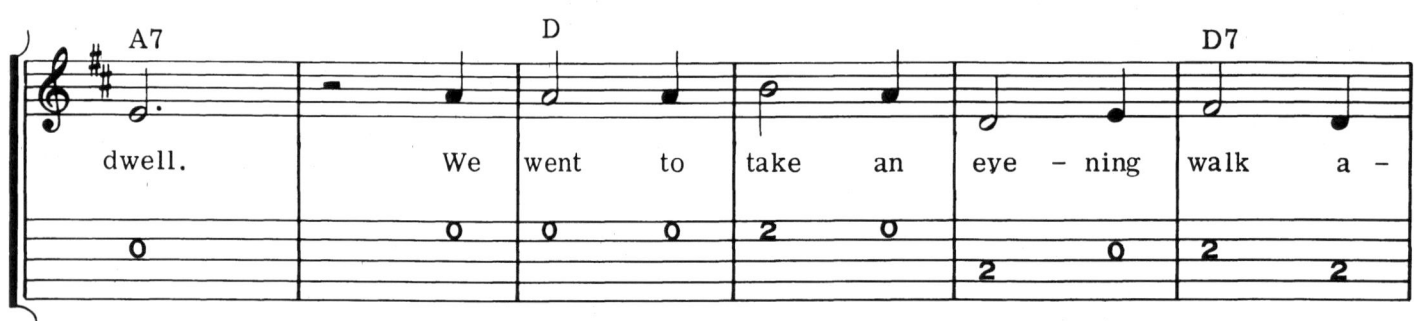
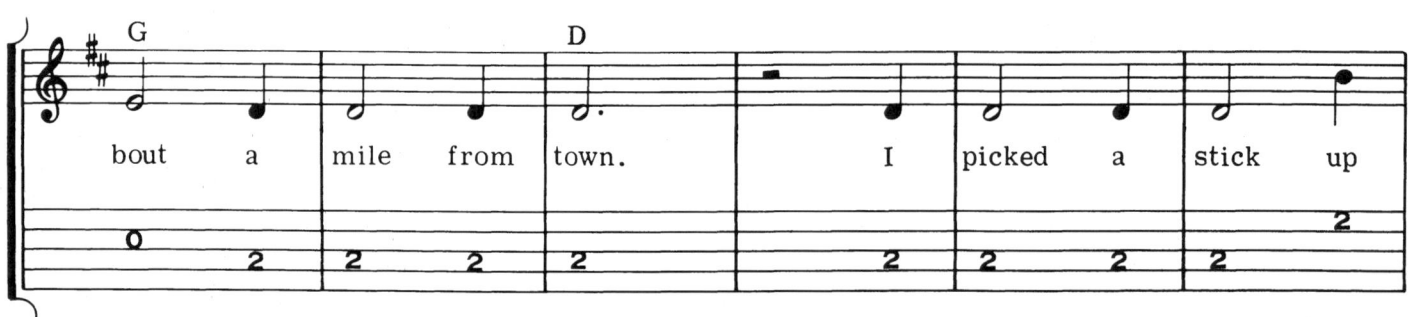
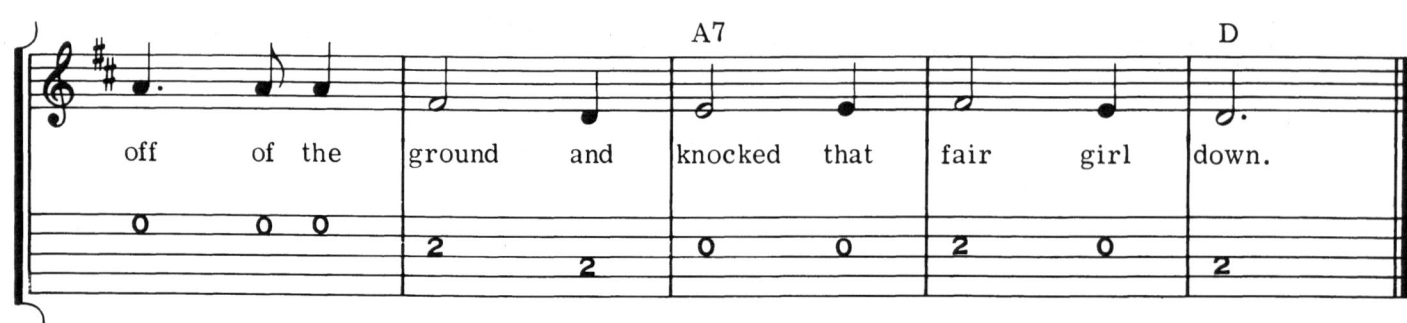

KNOXVILLE GIRL

THE BLUE-TAIL FLY

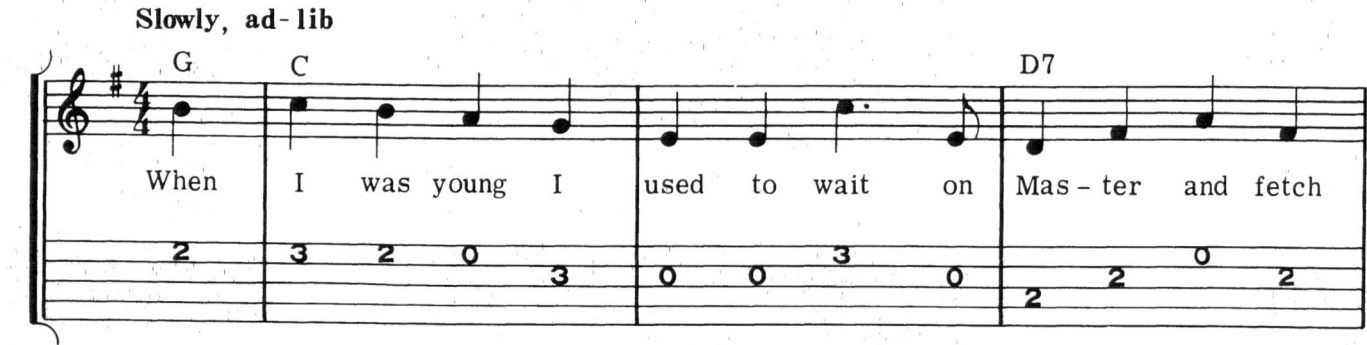
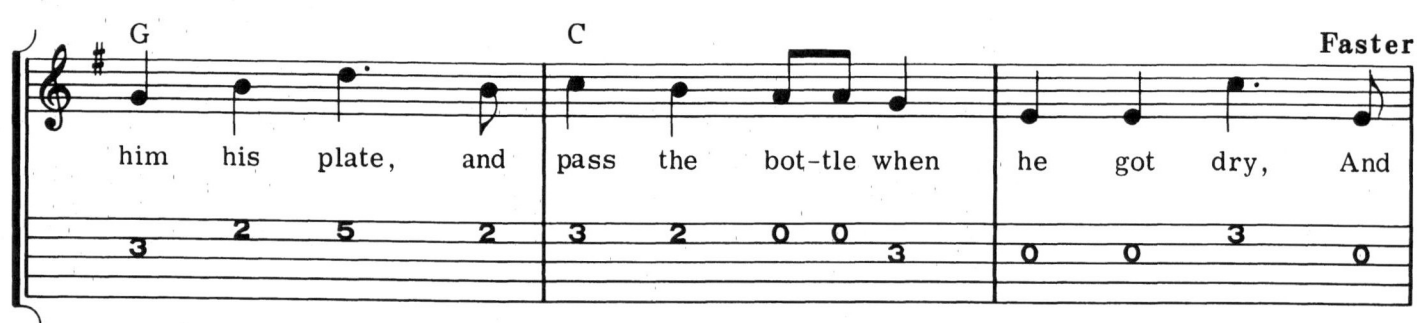

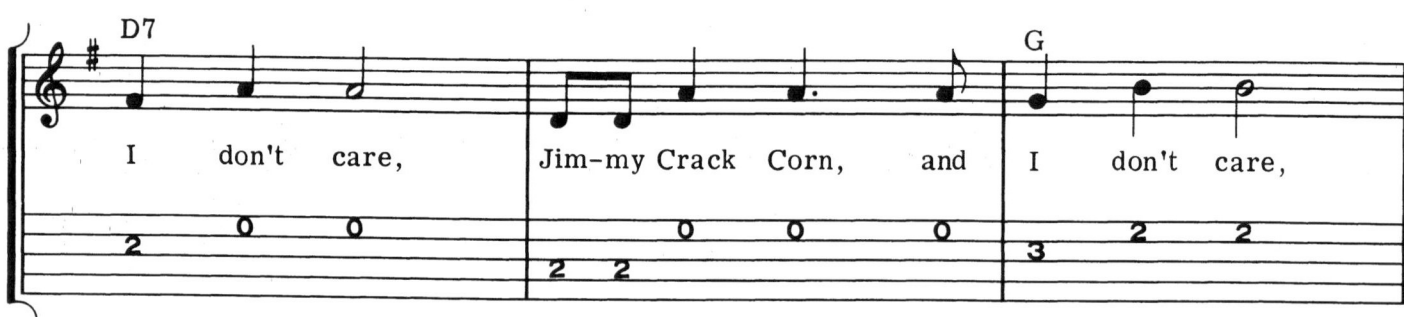

THE BLUE TAIL FLY

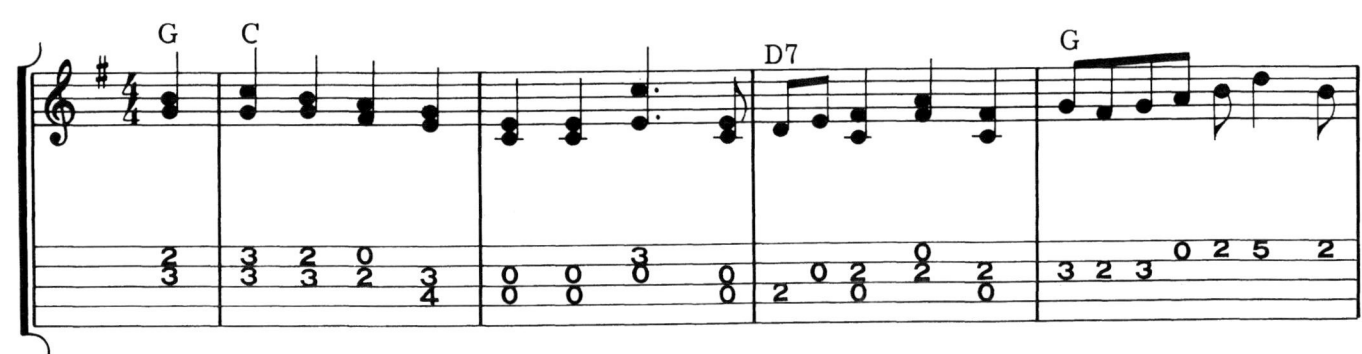

THE GIRL I LEFT BEHIND

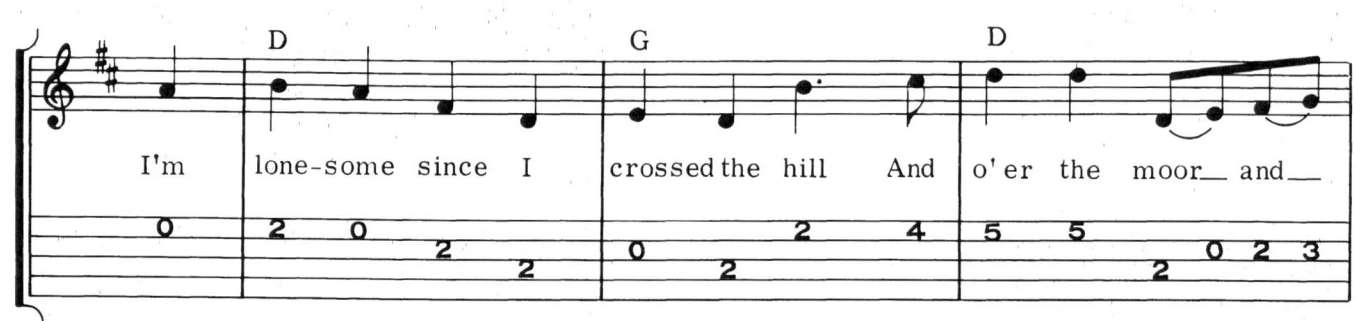
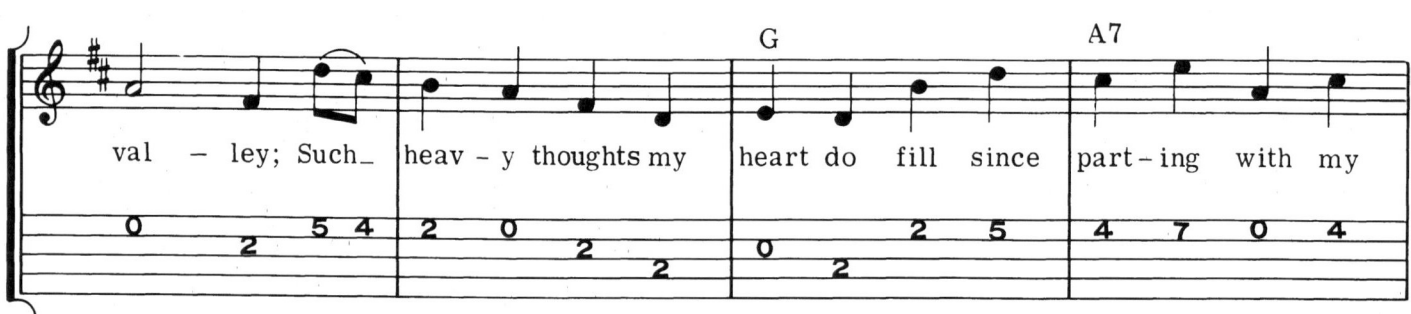
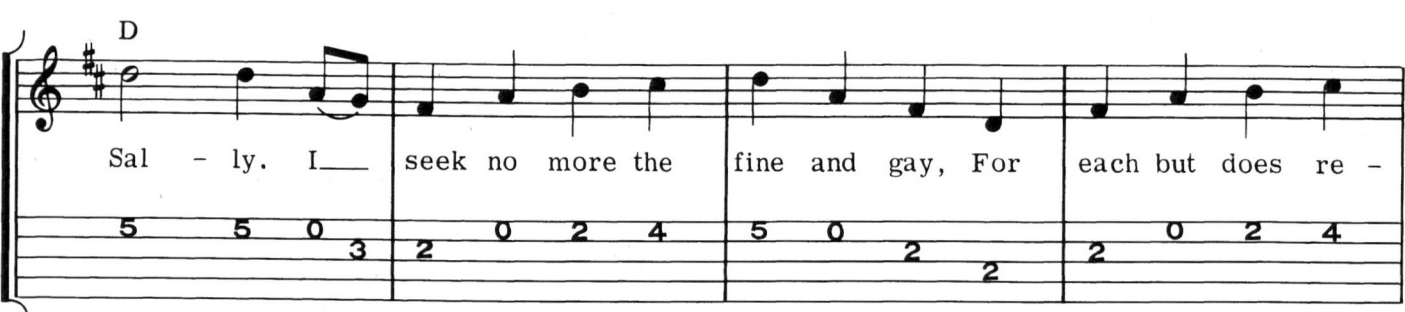
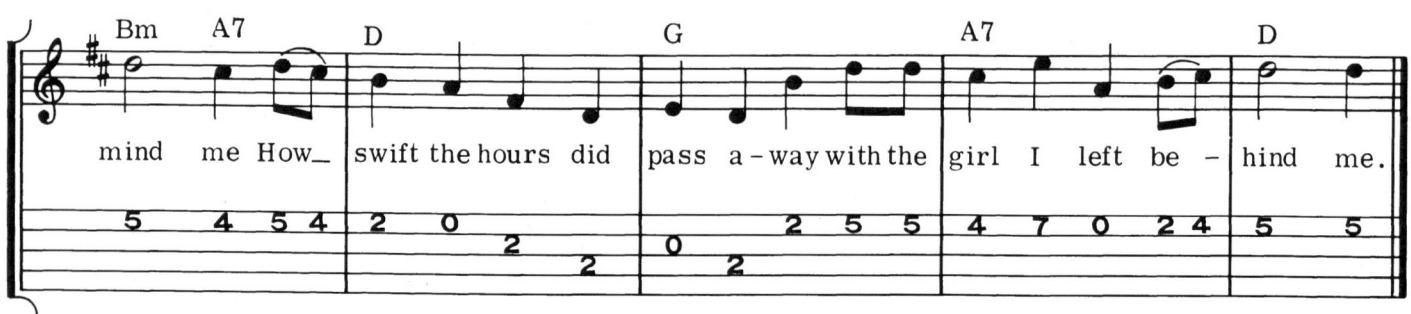

Oh ne'er shall I forget the night,
The stars were bright above me,
And gently lent their silv'ry light
When first she vowed to love me.
But now I'm bound across the sea,
So heaven guide me kindly
And send me safely back again
To the girl I left behind me.

THE GIRL I LEFT BEHIND

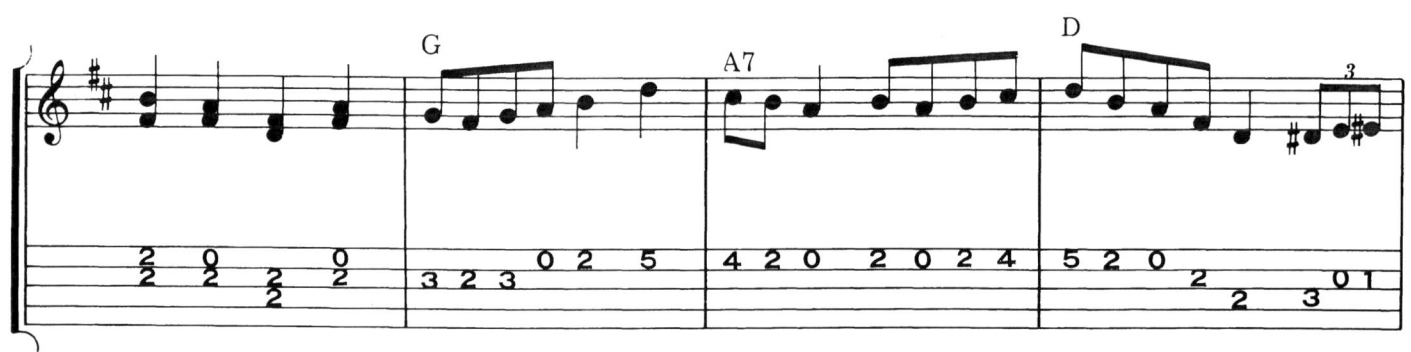

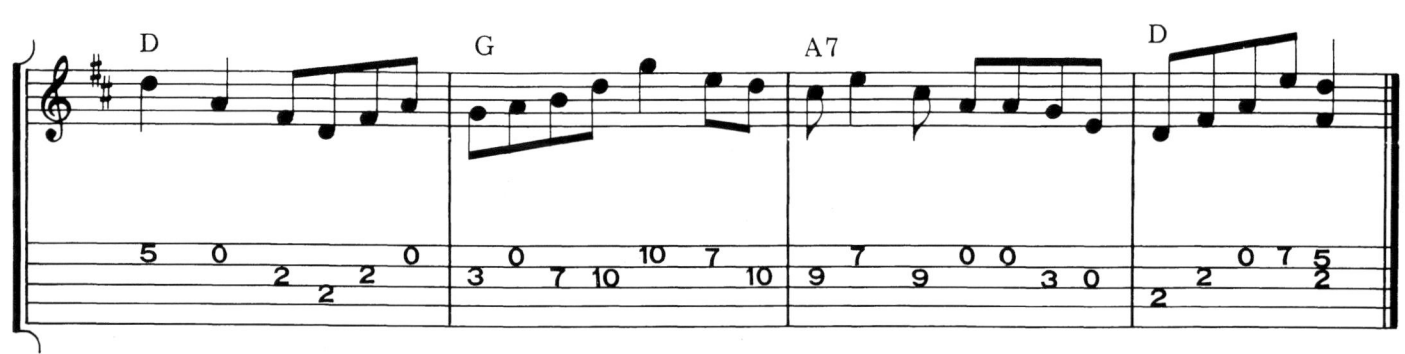

THE BIG ROCK CANDY MOUNTAIN

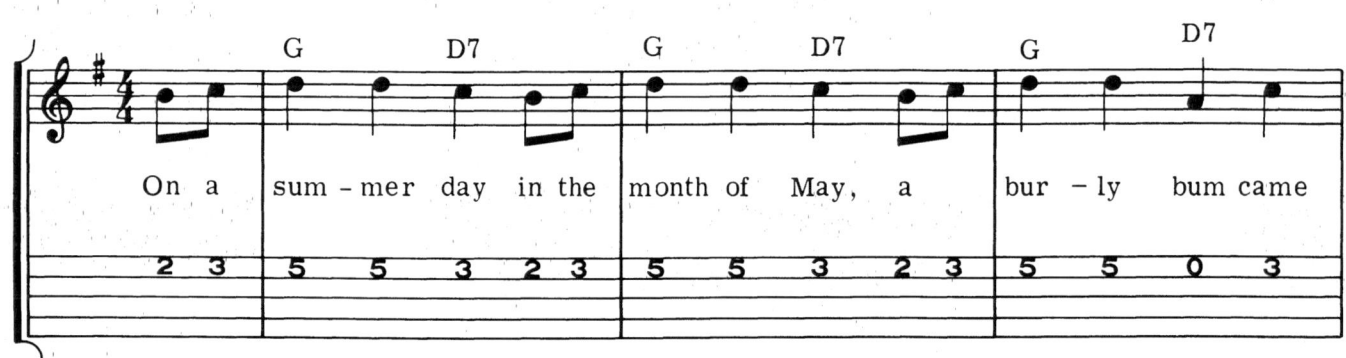

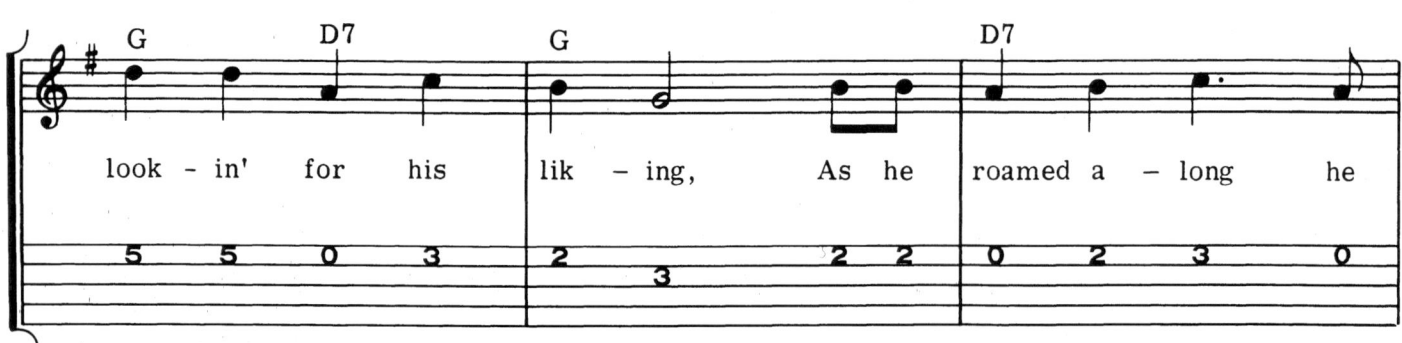
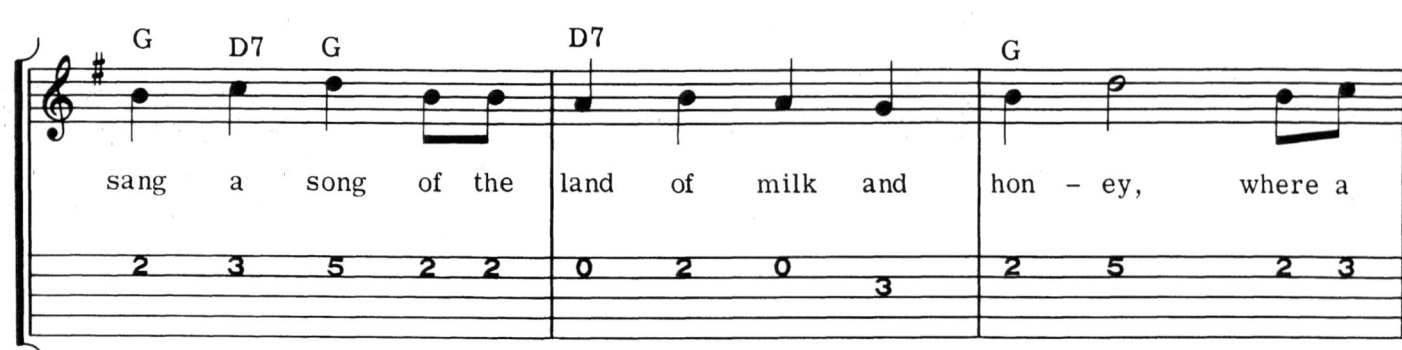

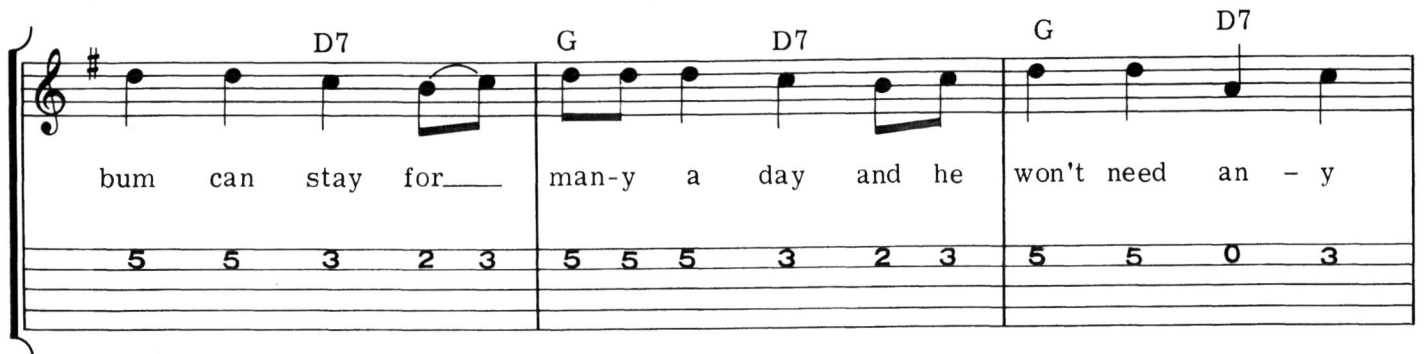

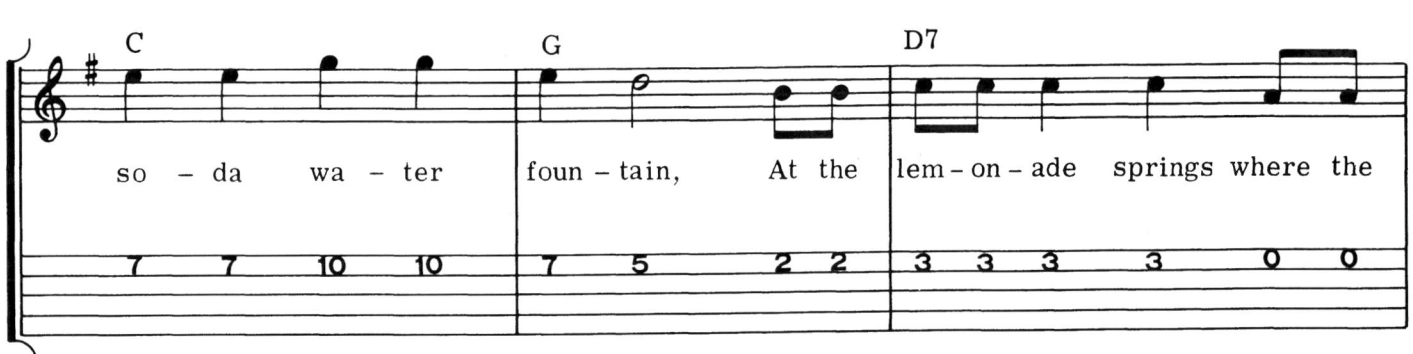
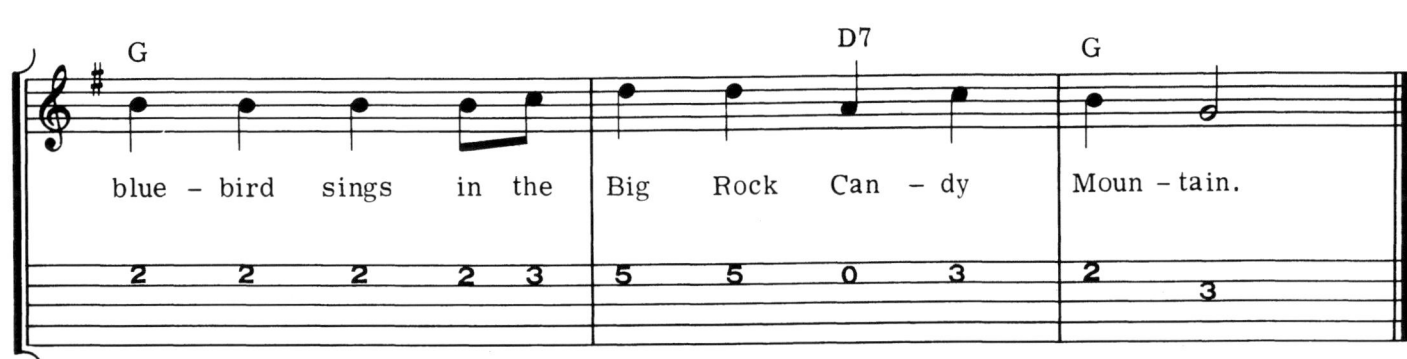

THE BIG ROCK CANDY MOUNTAIN

THE ASH GROVE

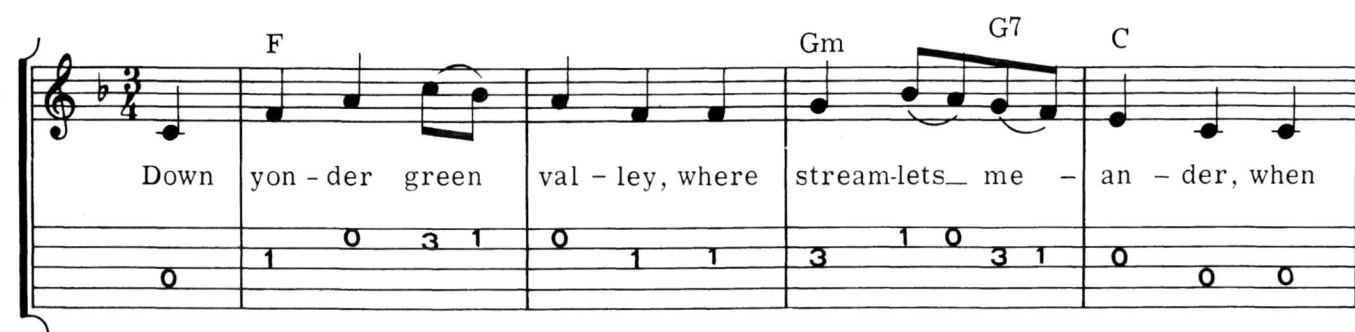
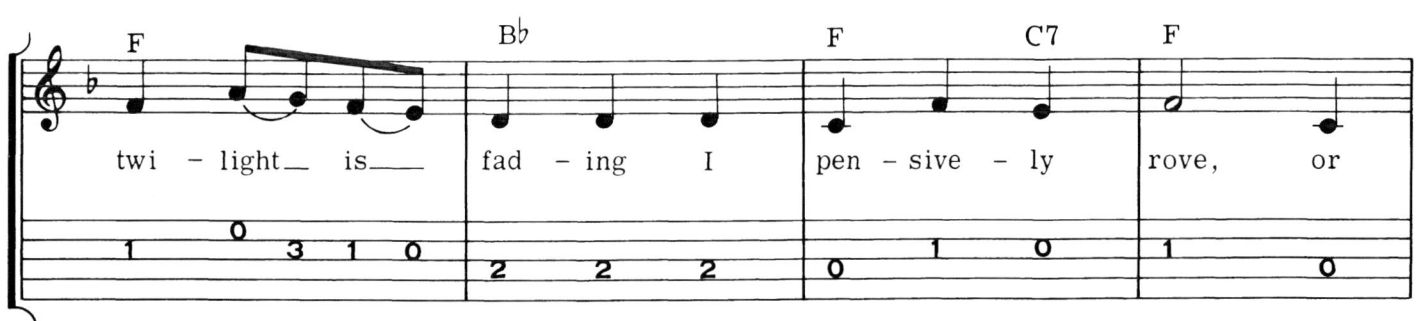
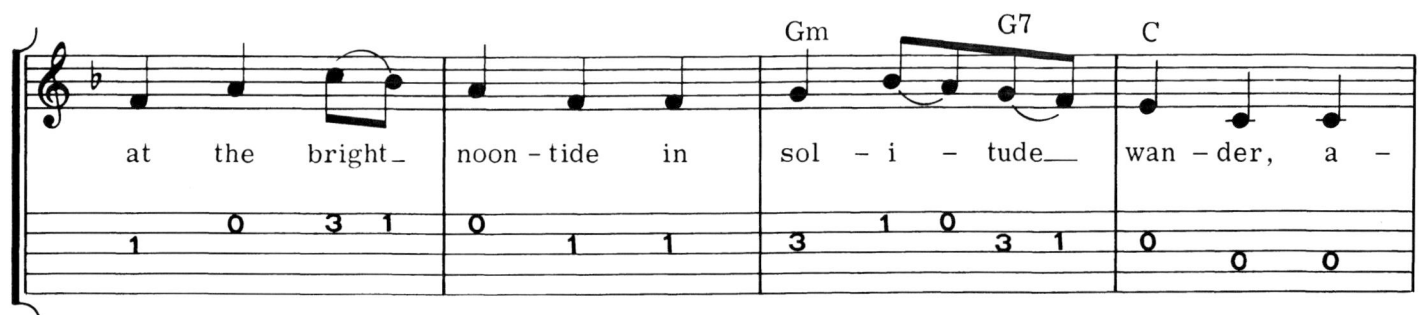
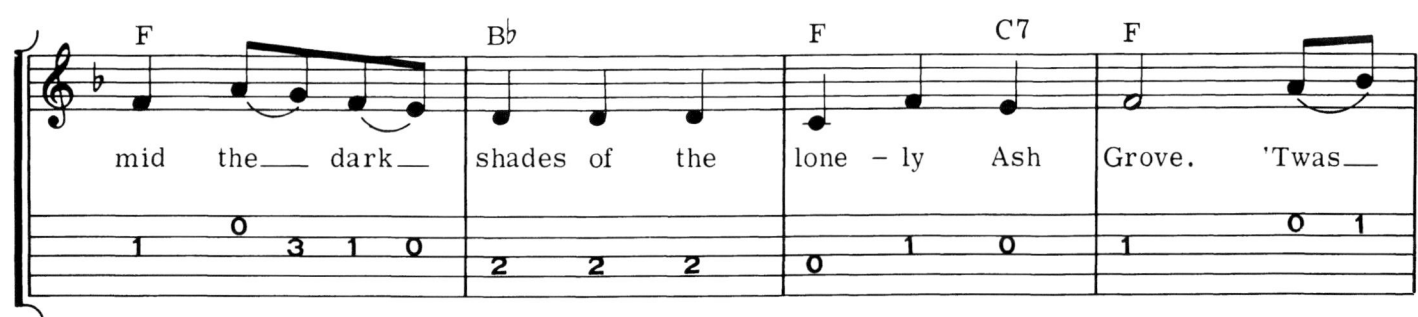
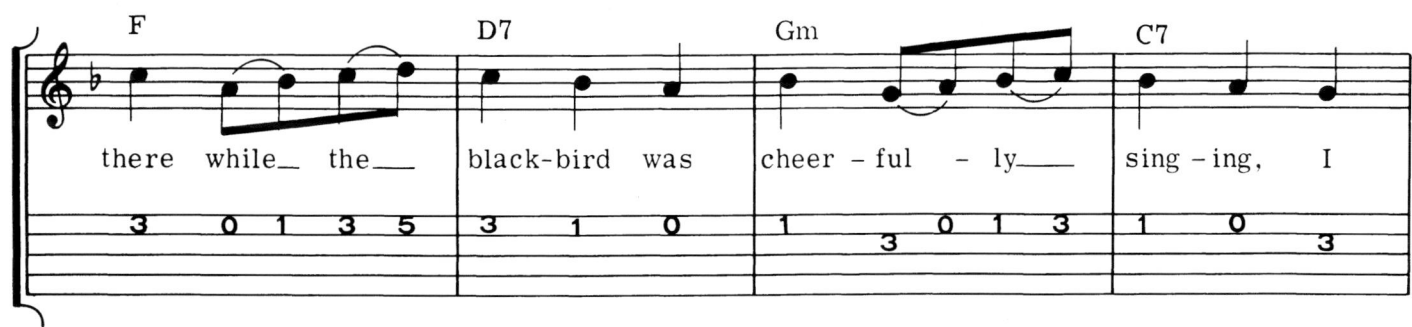

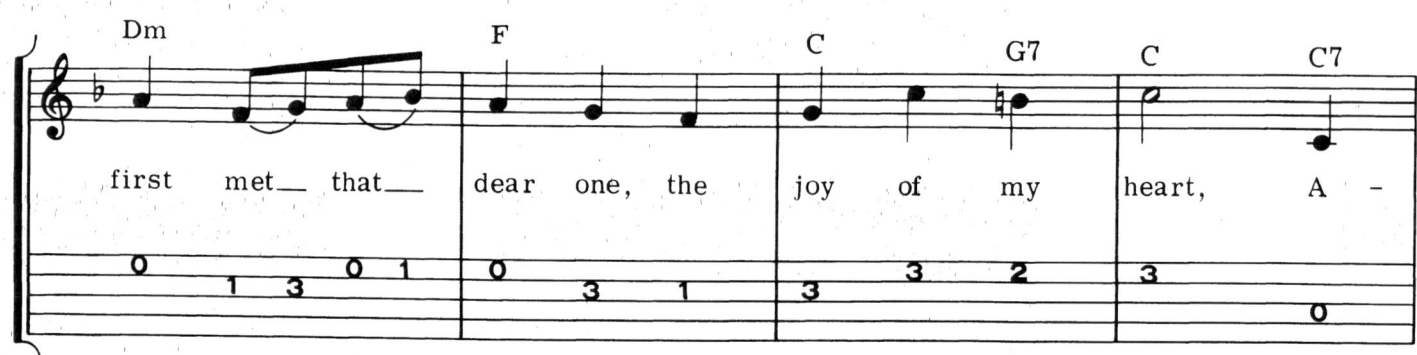

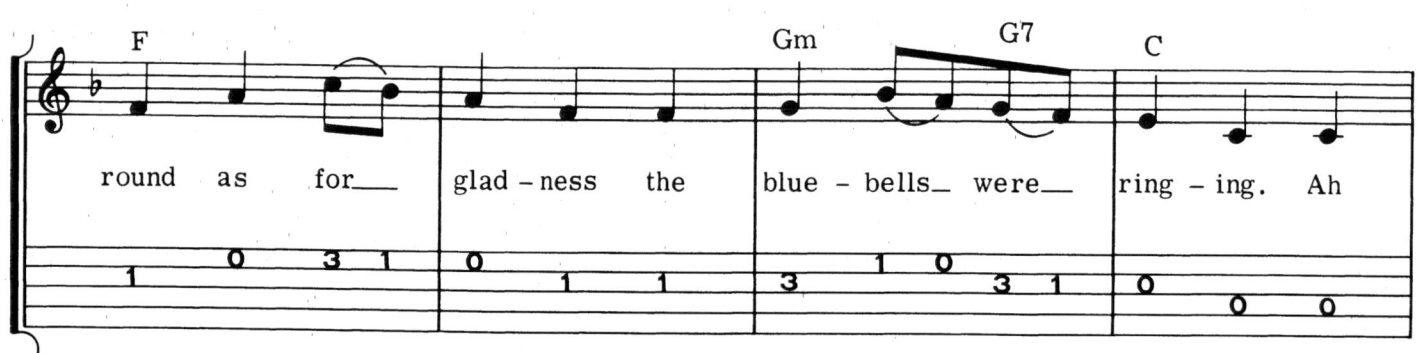

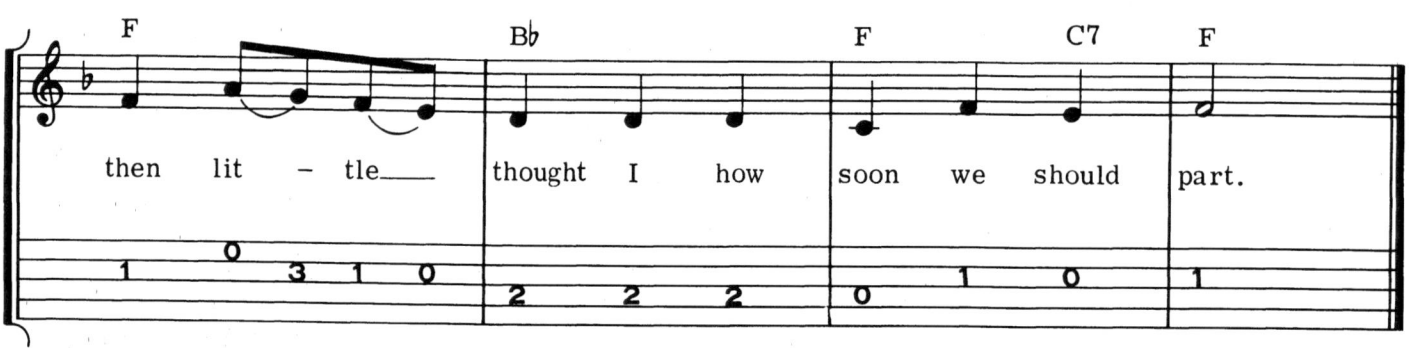

Still glows that bright sunshine o'er valley and mountain,
Still warbles the blackbird his note from the tree;
Still trembles the moonbeam on streamlet and fountain,
But what are the beauties of nature to me?

With sorrow, deep sorrow, my bosom is laden,
All day I go mourning in search of my love,
Ye echoes! Oh tell me where is the sweet maiden?
"She sleeps 'neath the green turf down by the Ash Grove."

THE ASH GROVE

HOME ON THE RANGE

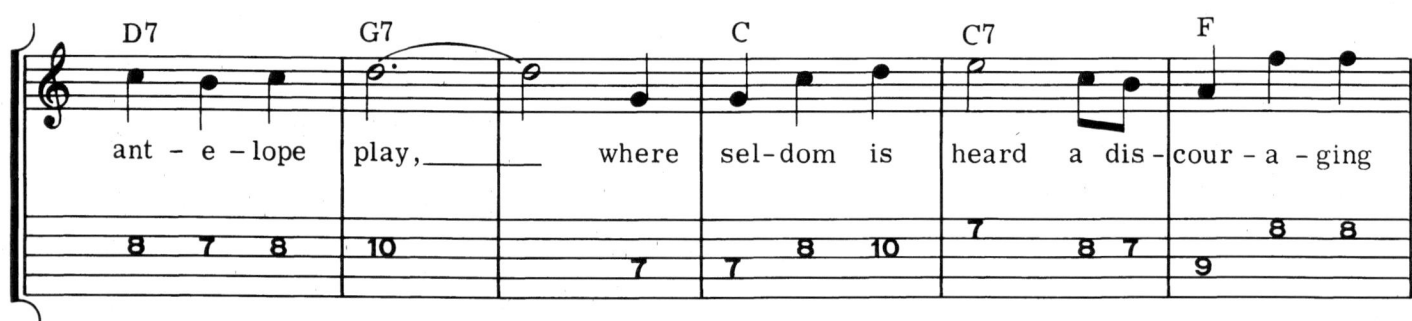
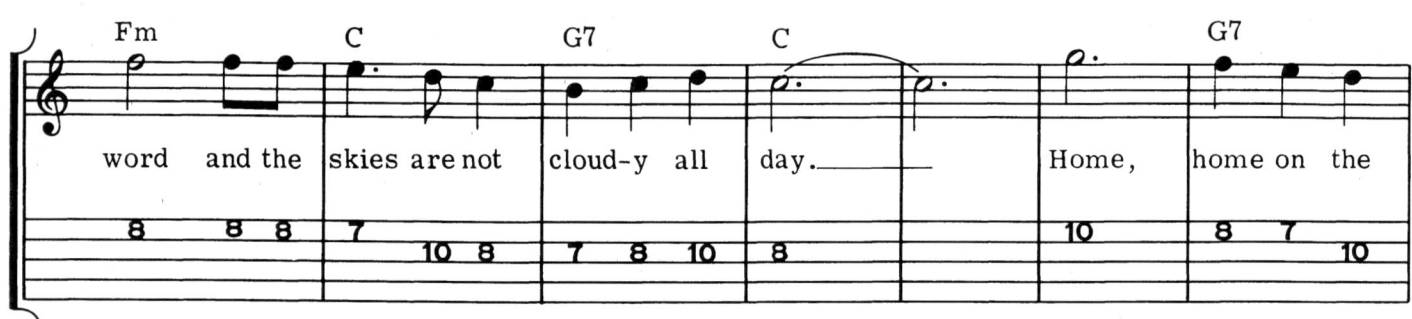
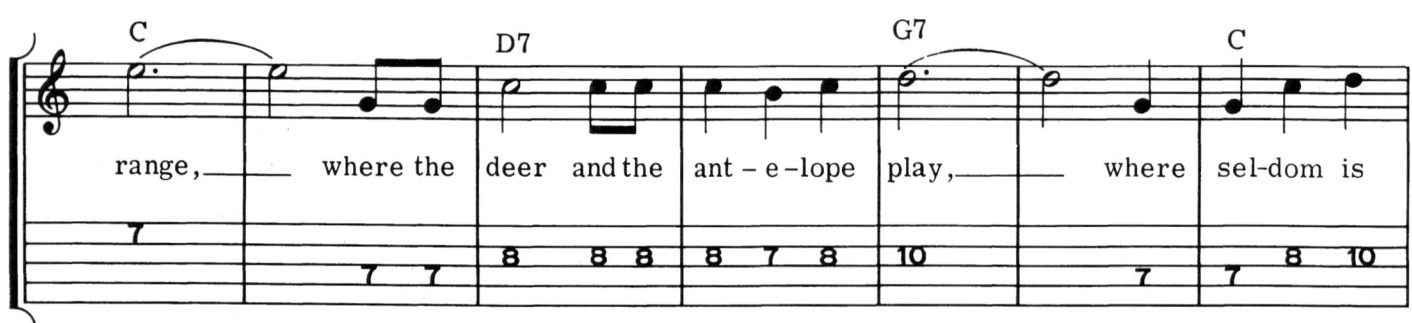
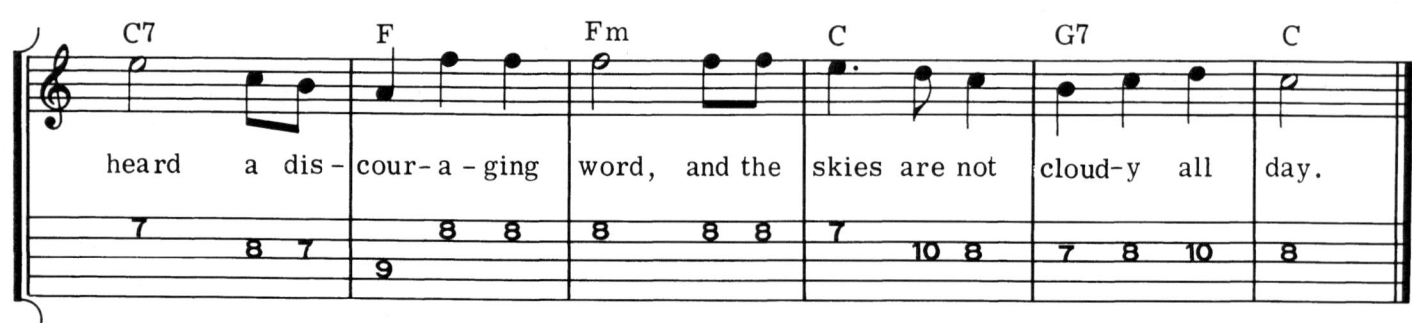

HOME ON THE RANGE

BLOW, YE WINDS

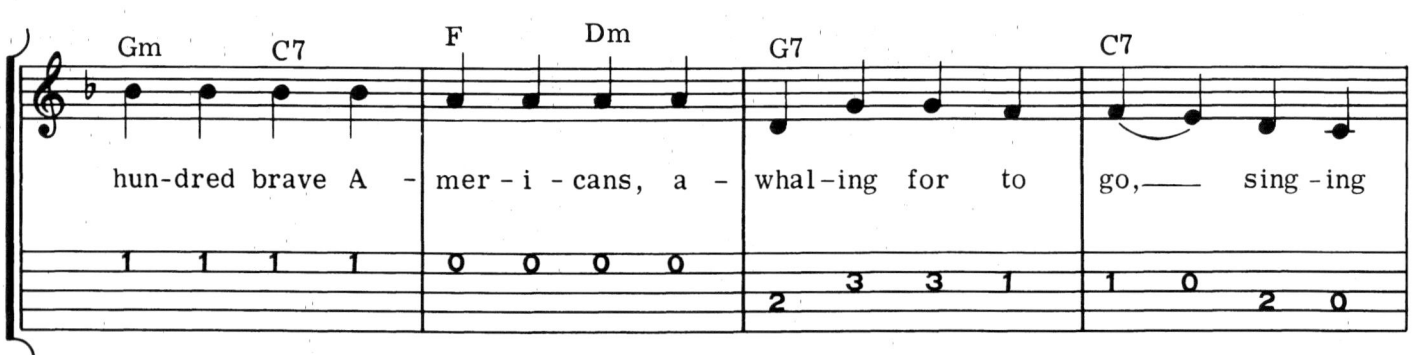
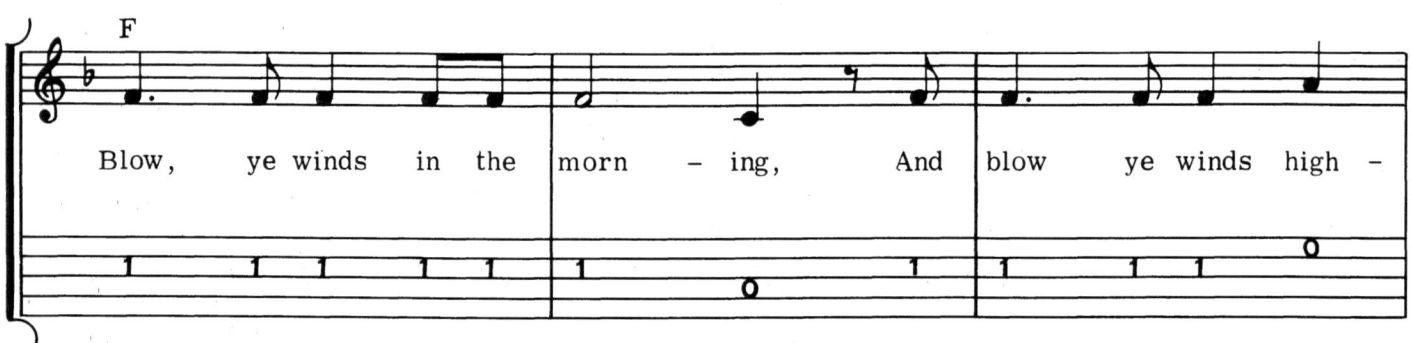
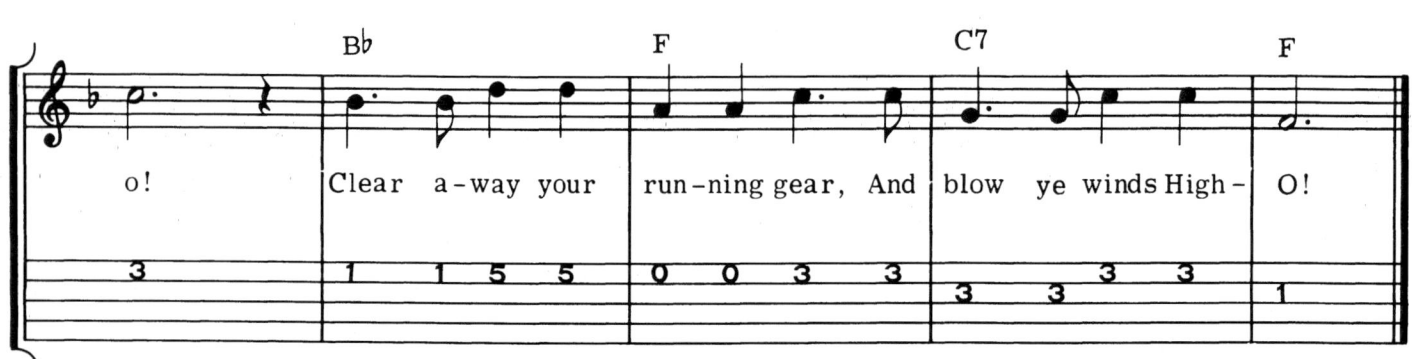

BLOW, YE WINDS

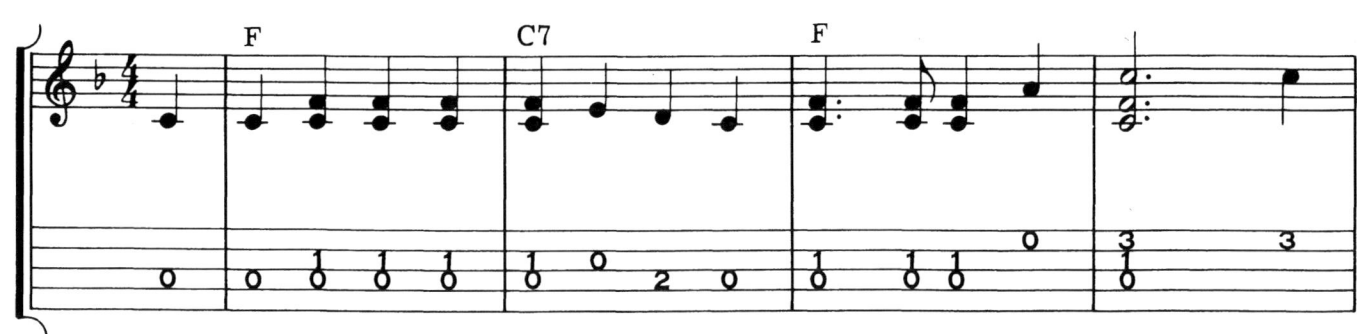
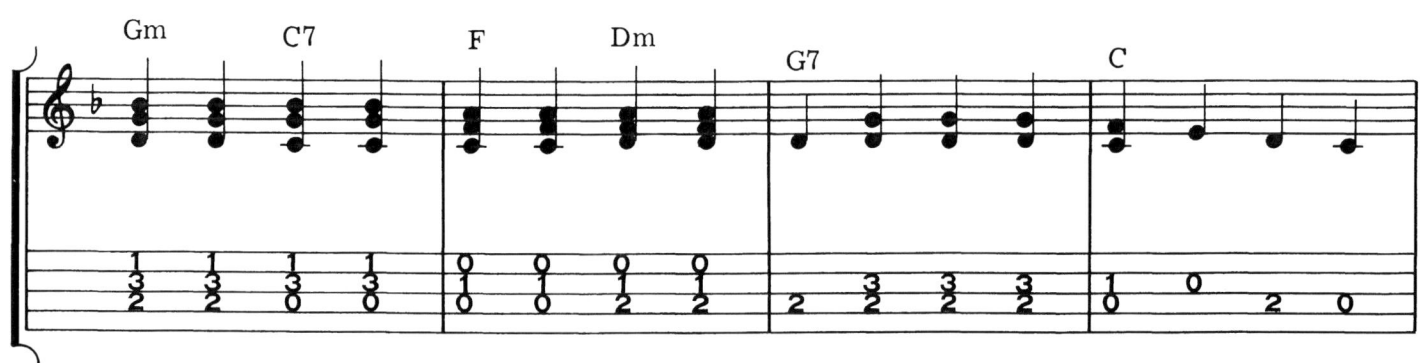

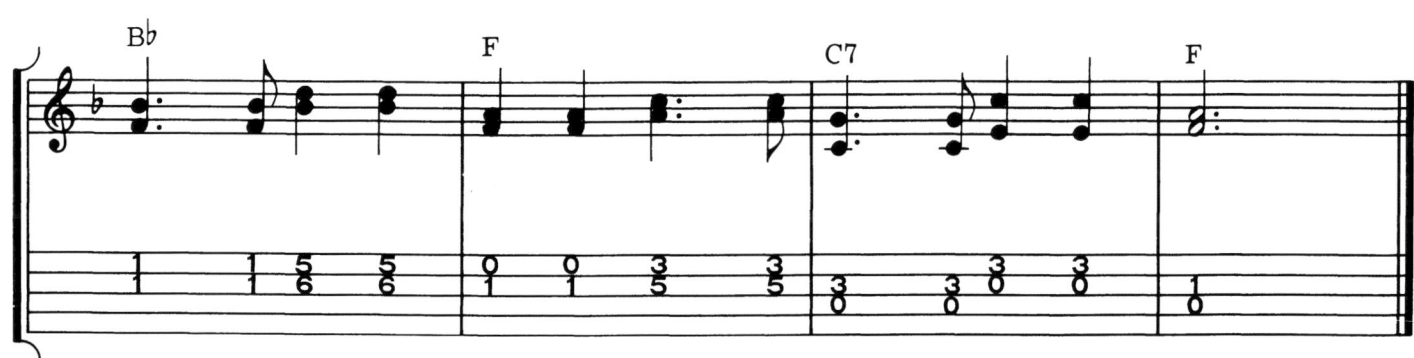

SWEET BETSY FROM PIKE

The Shanghai ran off and their cattle all died;
That morning the last piece of bacon was fried;
Poor Ike was discouraged, and Betsy got mad,
The dog drooped his tail and looked wondrously sad.

SWEET BETSY FROM PIKE

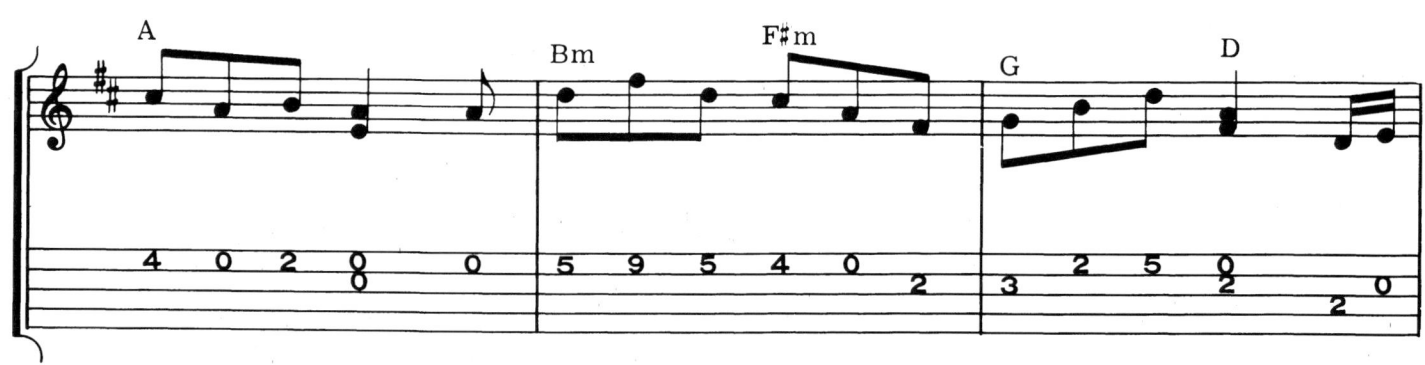
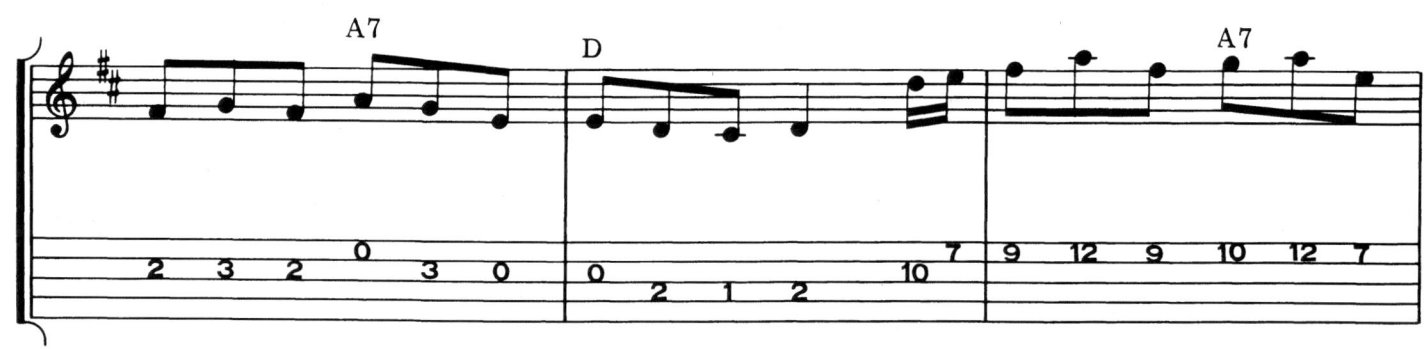
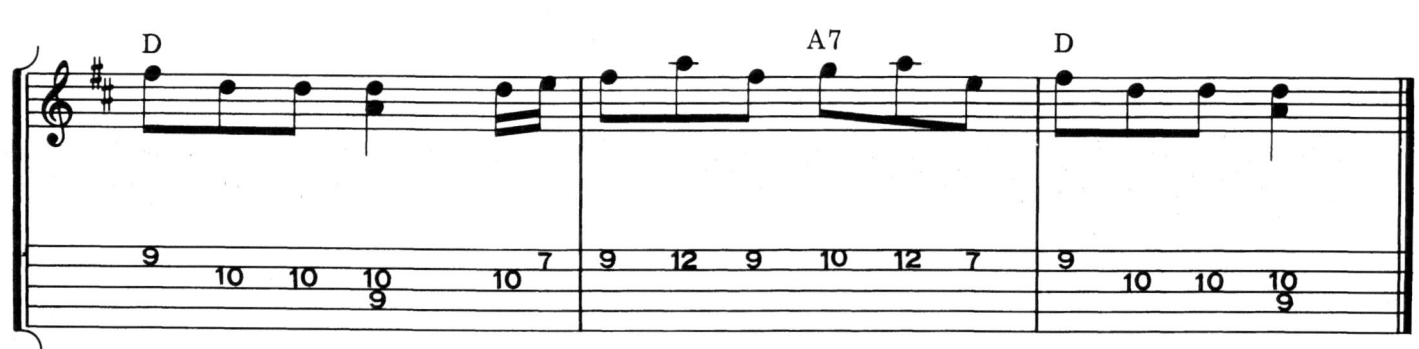

DOWN IN THE VALLEY

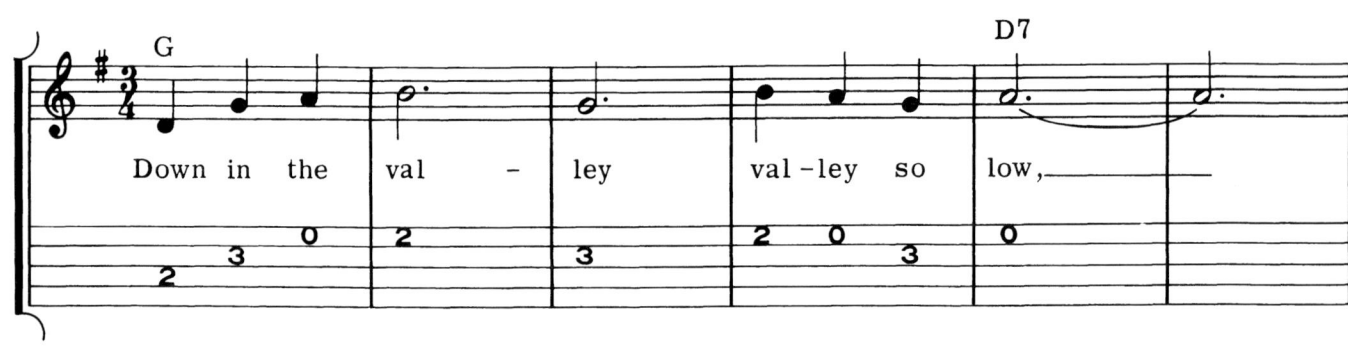

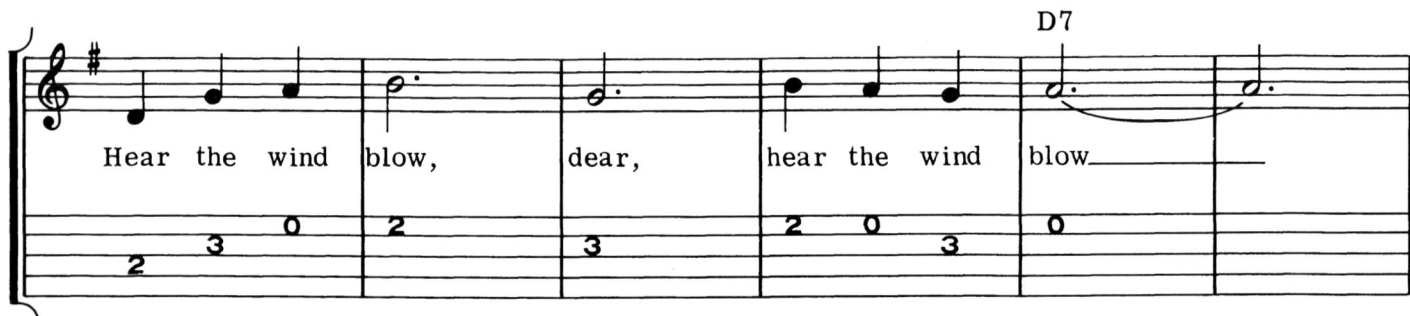
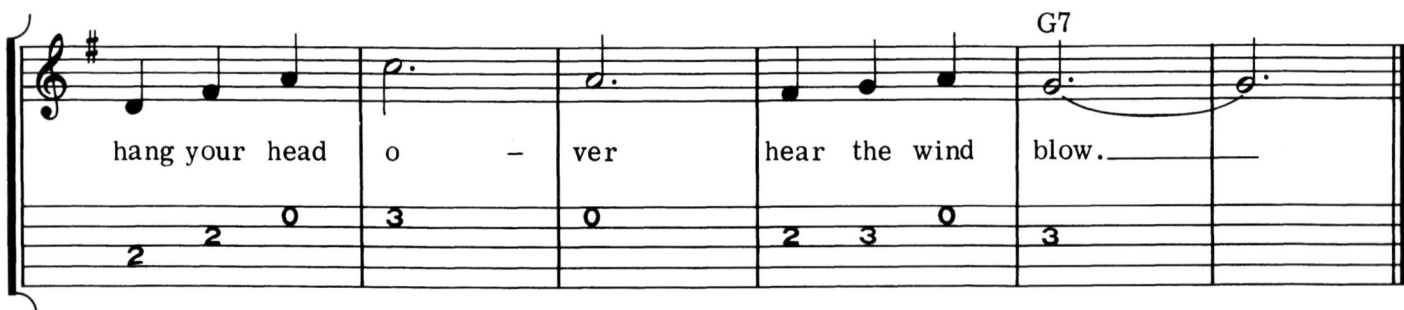

Build me a castle, forty feet high,
So I can see her as she goes by.
As she goes by dear, as she goes by,
So I can see her as she goes by.

DOWN IN THE VALLEY

LITTLE BROWN JUG

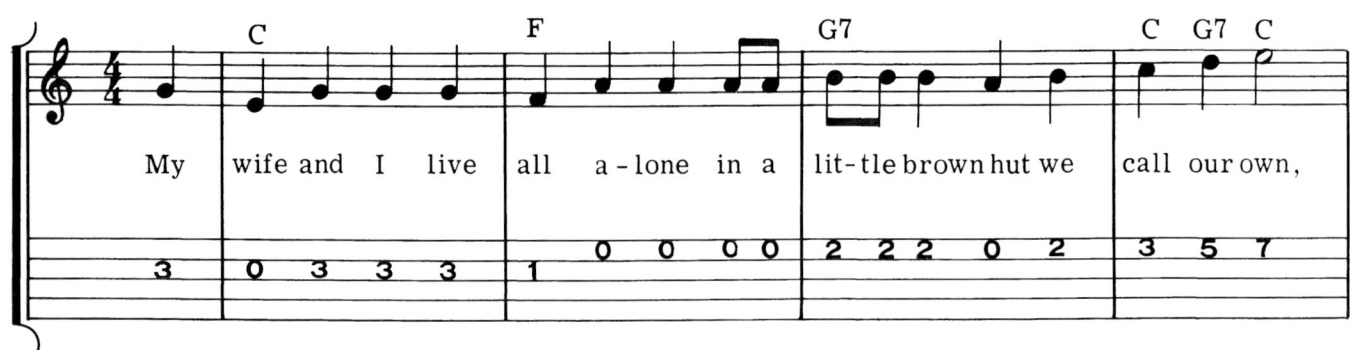

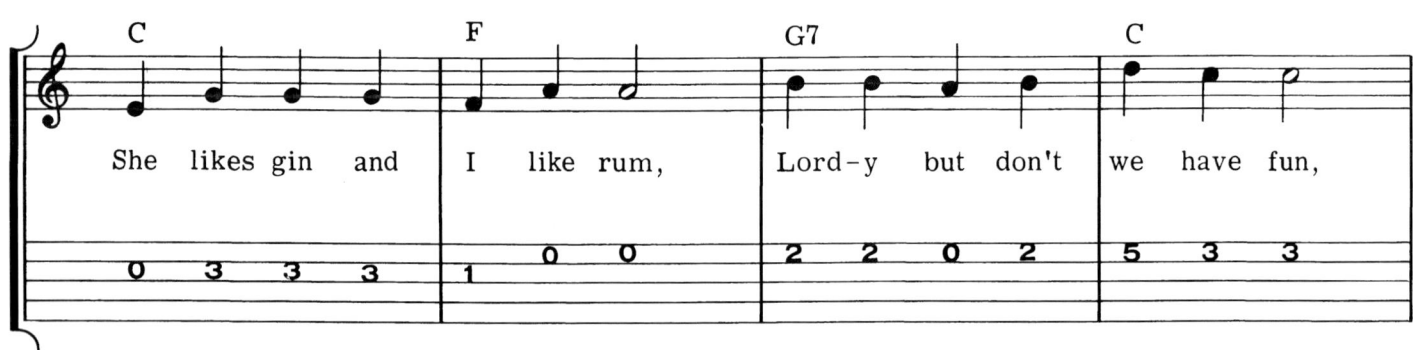

Chorus

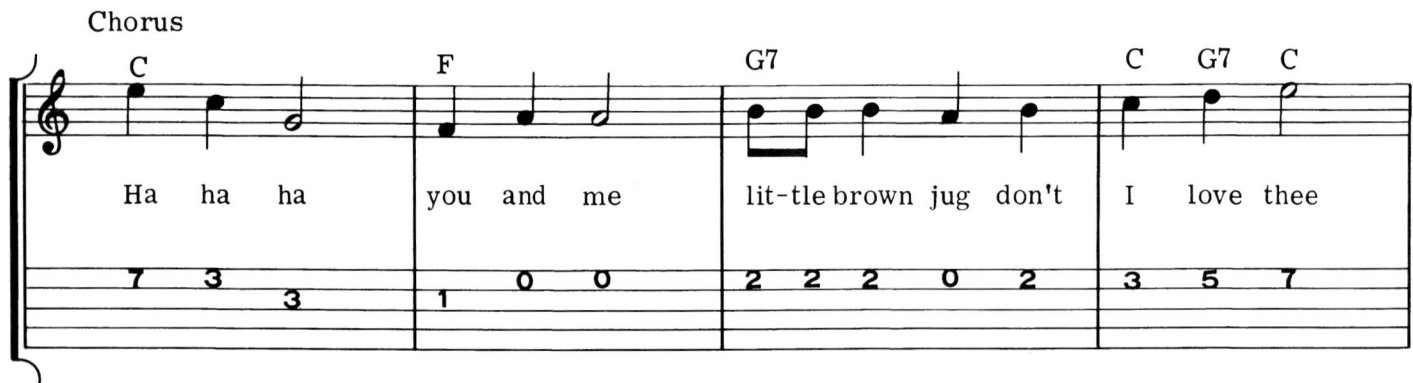

LITTLE BROWN JUG

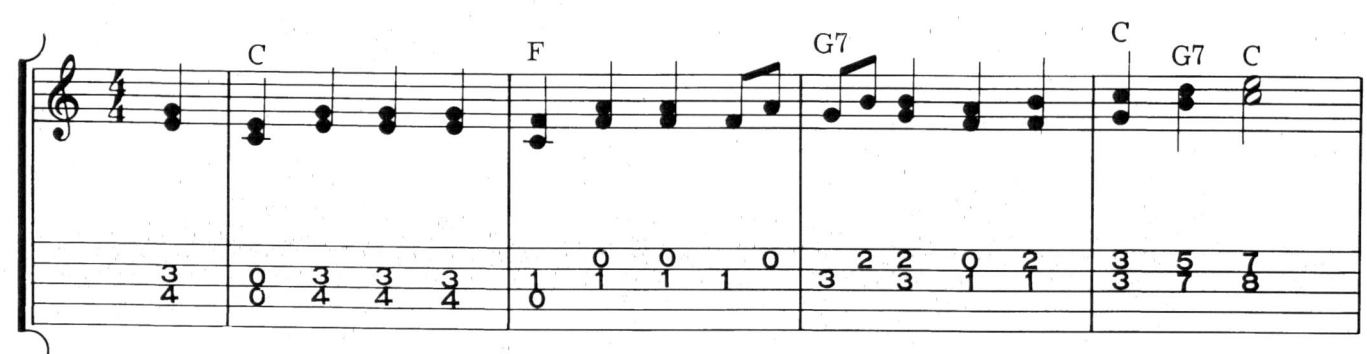
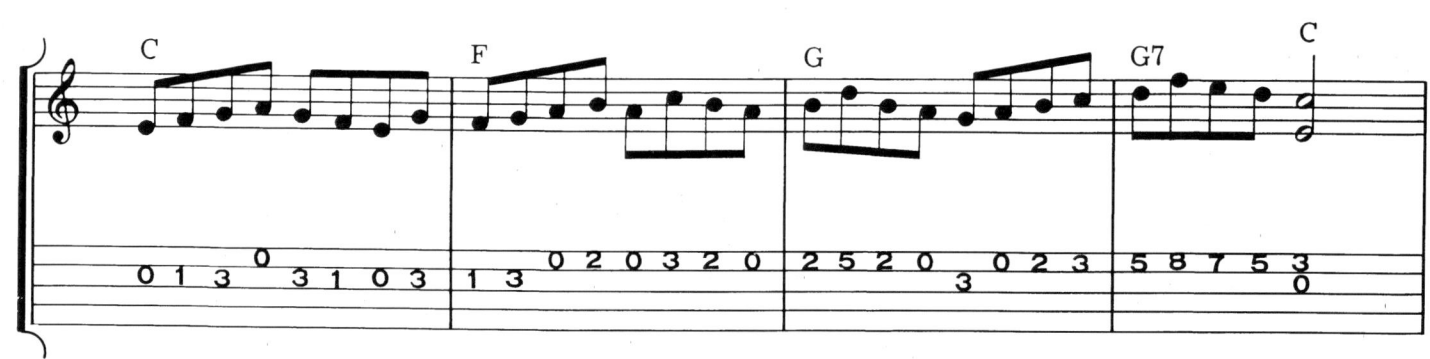
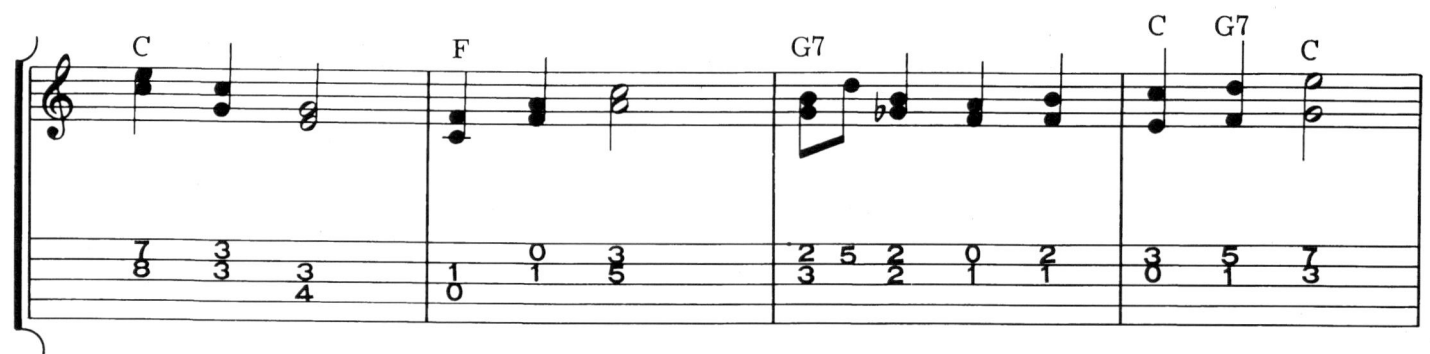
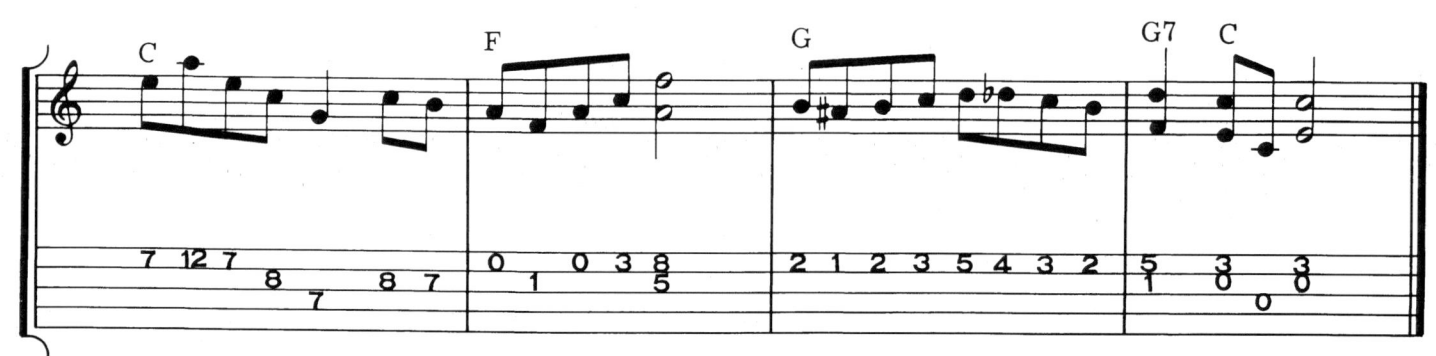

OH SUZANNA

OH SUZANNA

SHENANDOAH

Oh Shenandoah, I love your daughter, Away, you rolling river,
Oh Shenandoah, I love your daughter,
Away, we're bound away, 'cross the wide Missouri.

Farewell my dear, I'm bound to leave you, away you rolling river,
Oh Senandoah, I'll not deceive you.
Away, we're bound away, 'cross the wide Missouri.

SHENANDOAH

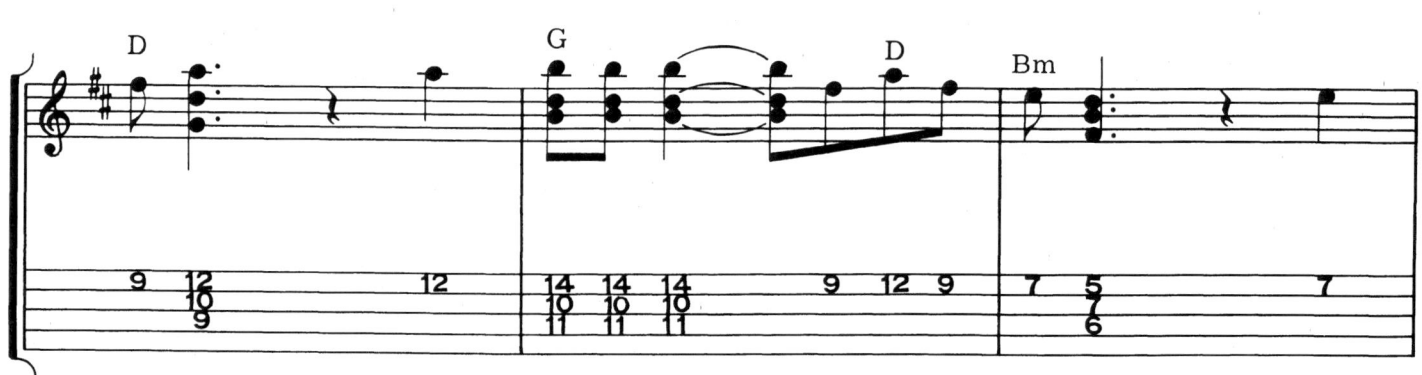
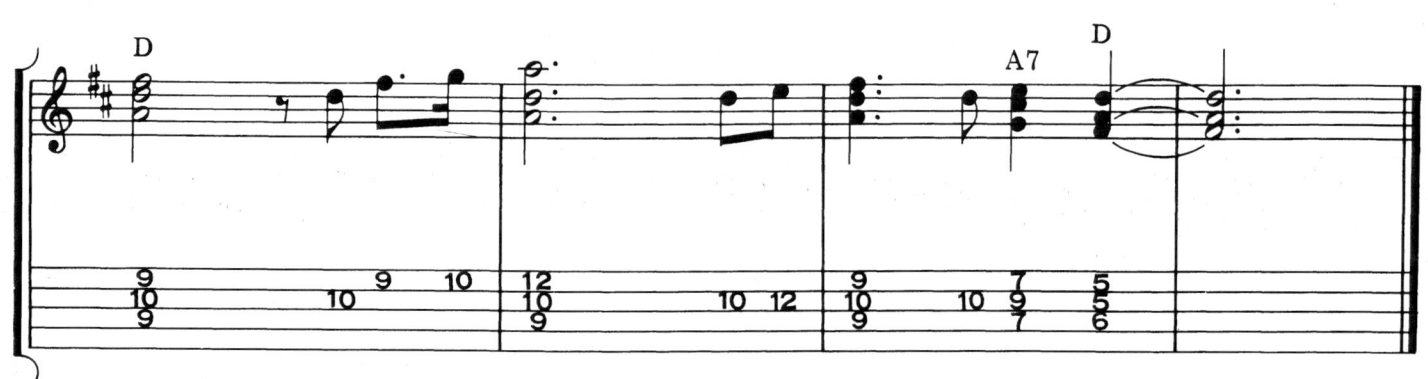

TURKEY IN THE STRAW

TURKEY IN THE STRAW

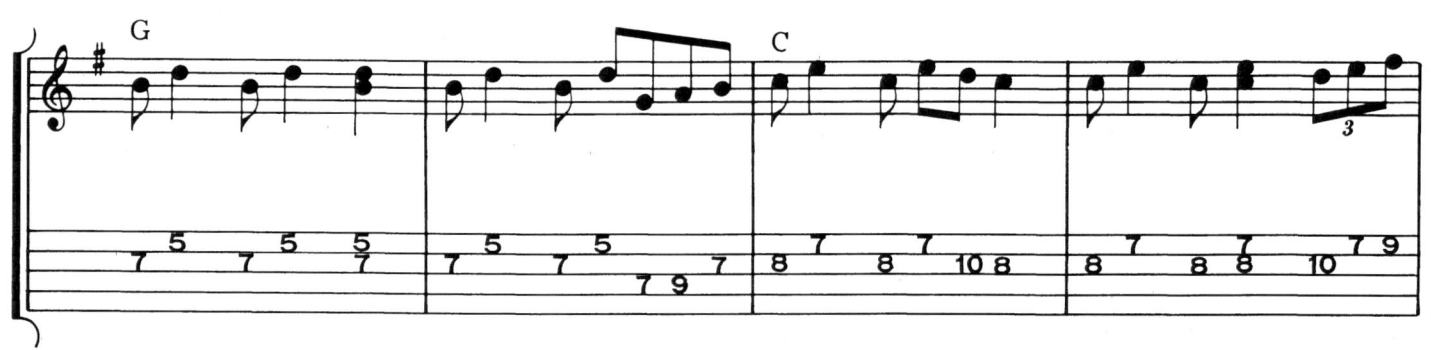
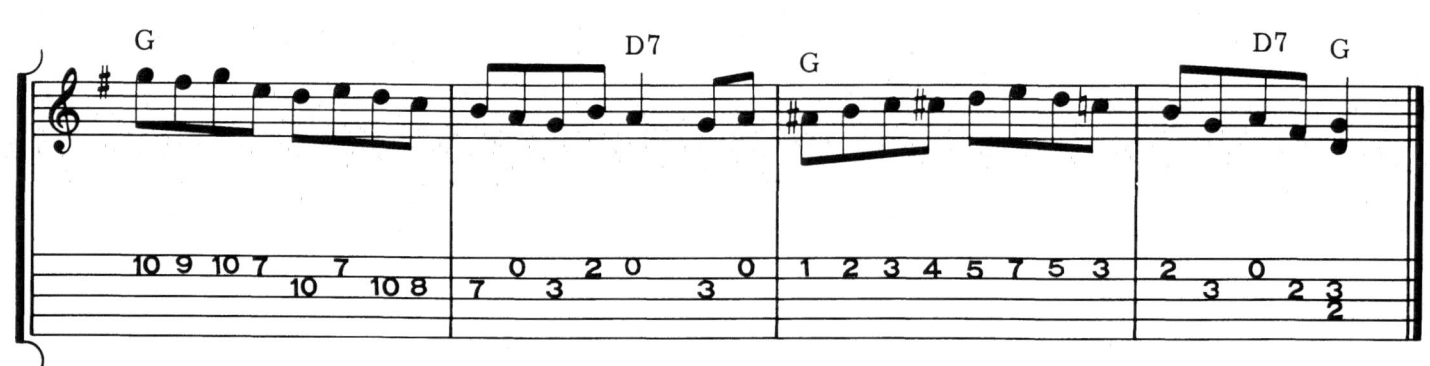

THERE IS A TAVERN IN THE TOWN

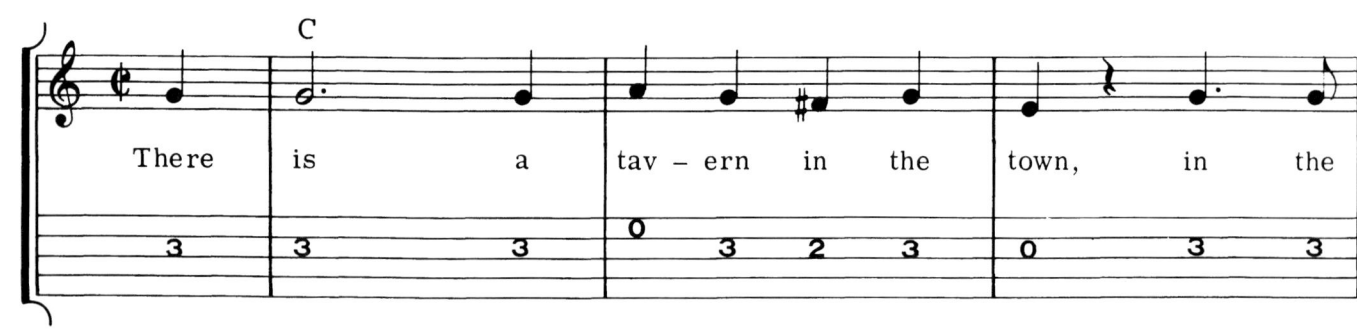

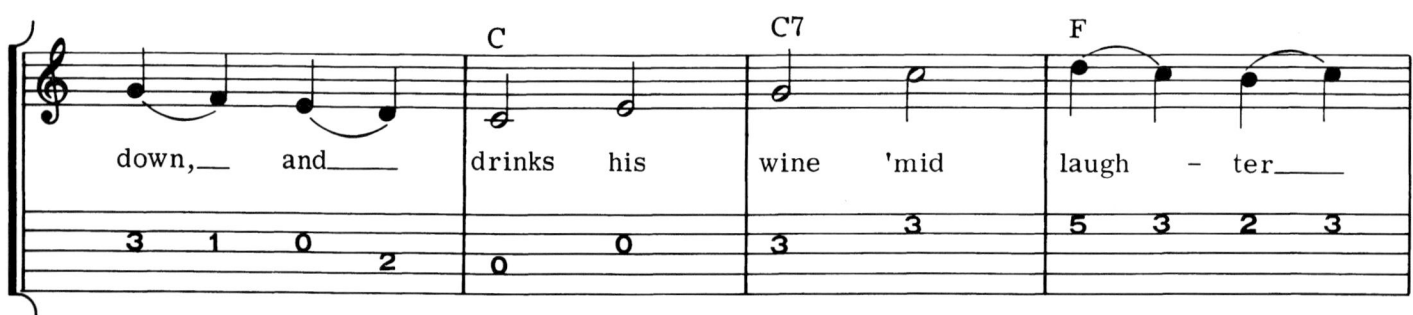
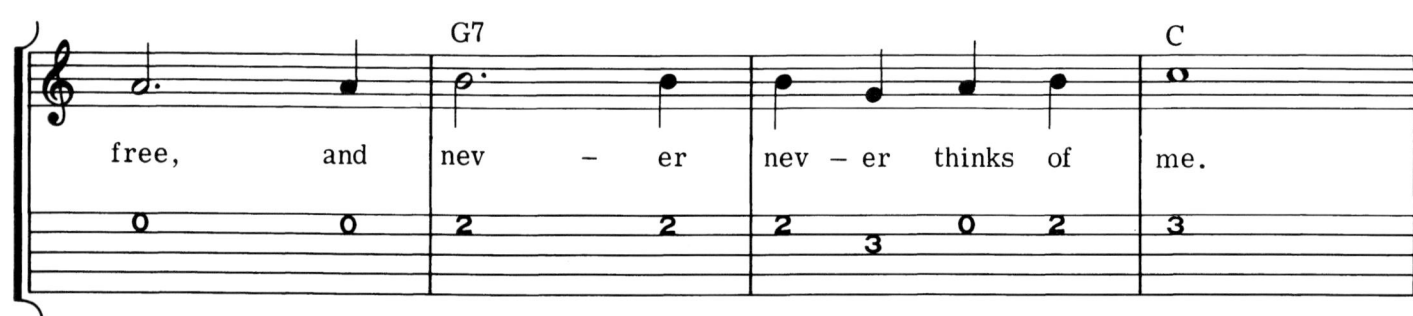

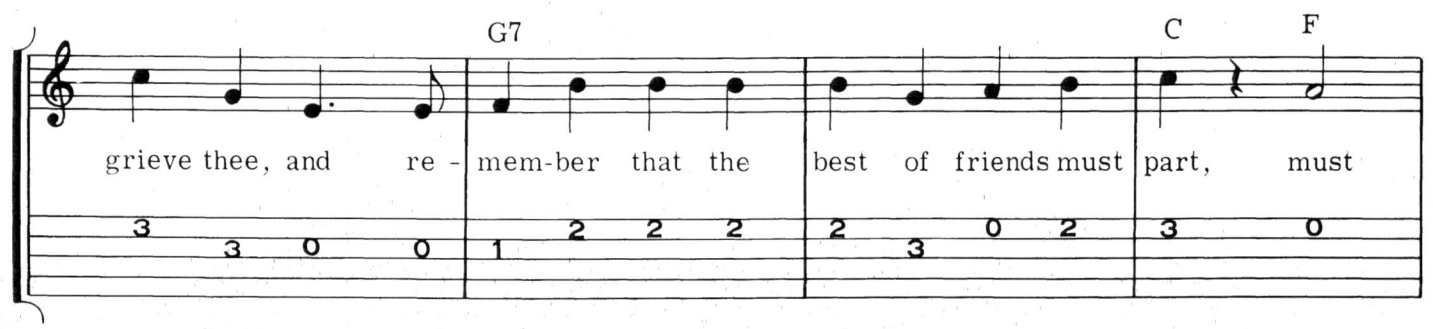

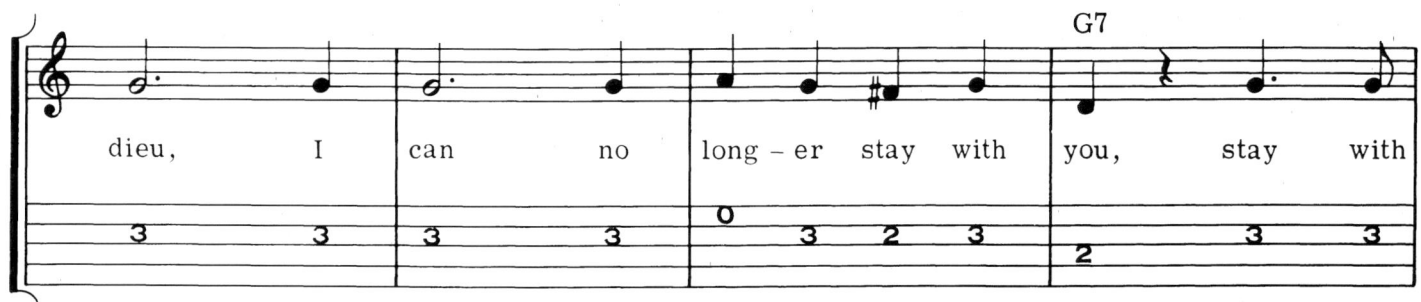
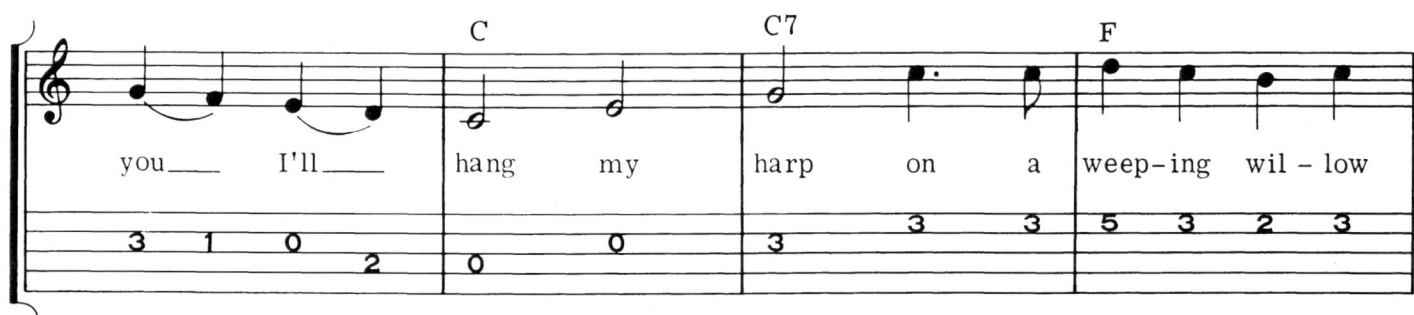
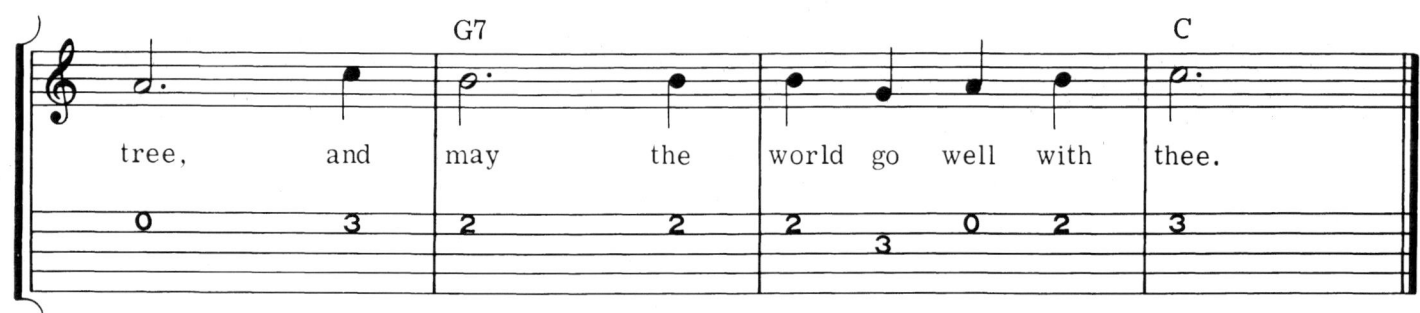

THERE IS A TAVERN IN THE TOWN

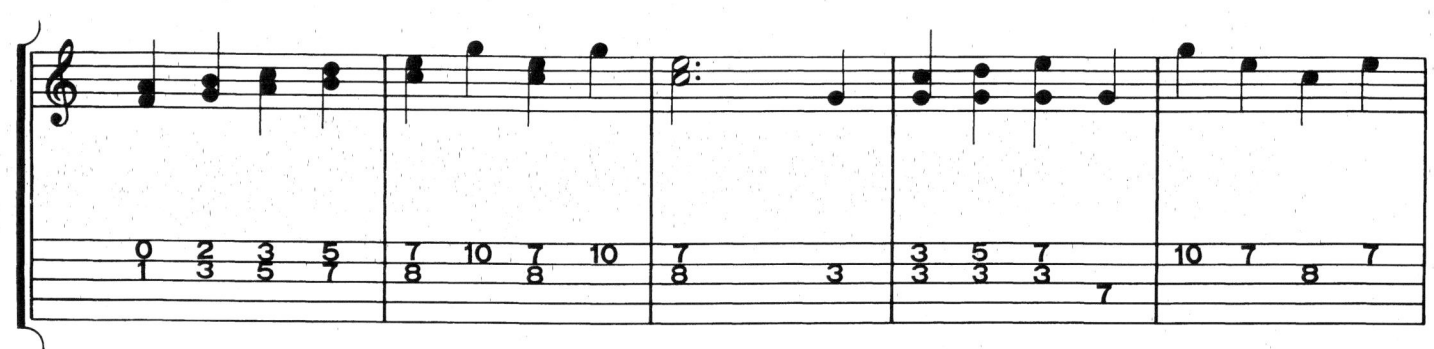

RIO GRANDE

RIO GRANDE

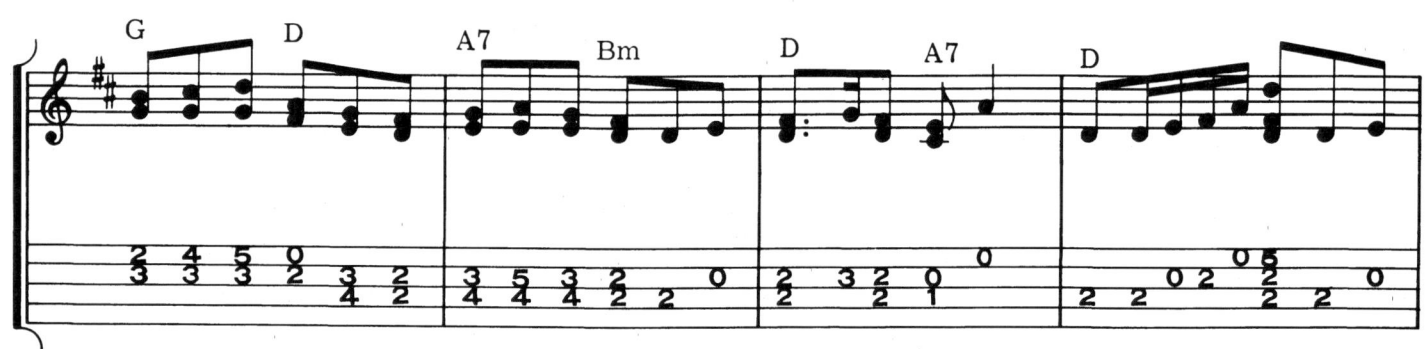

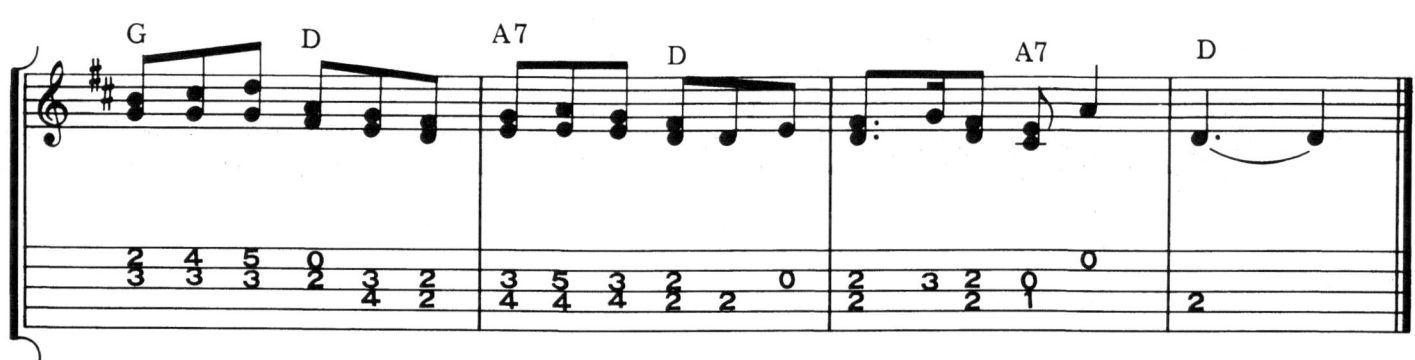

JOHN HARDY

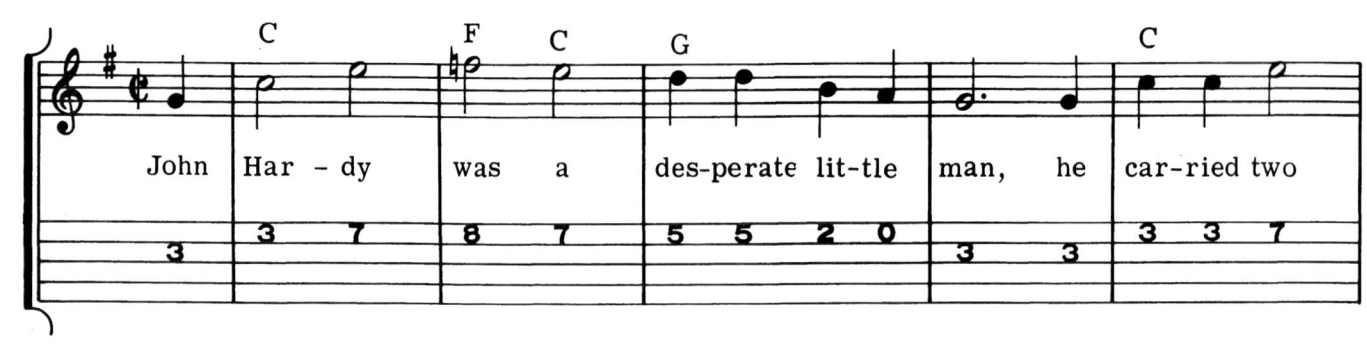
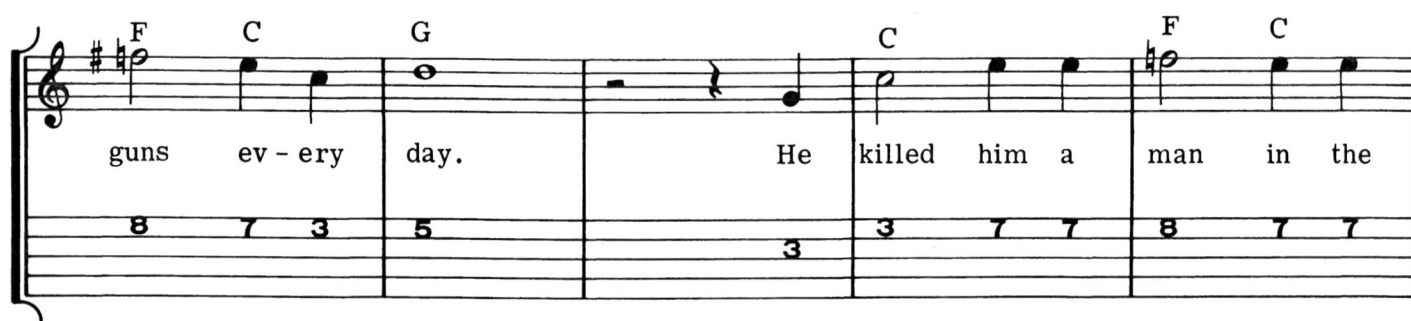
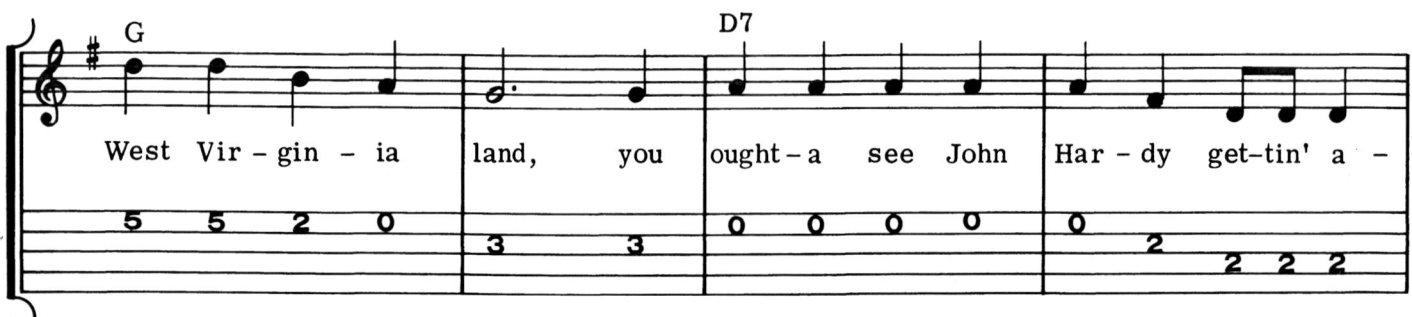
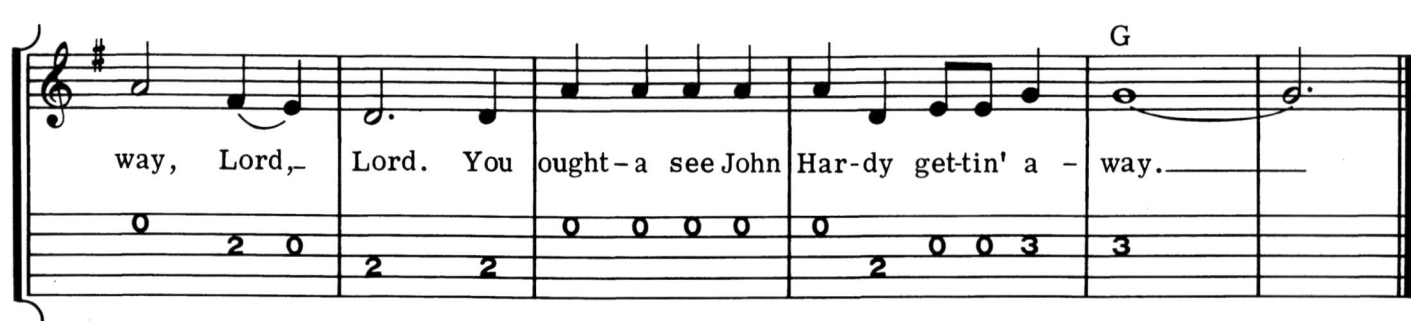

They took John Hardy to the hangin' ground,
They took him there to die,
The very last words that poor boy said,
"My forty-five never told a lie, Lord, Lord.
My forty-five never told a lie."

JOHN HARDY

RED RIVER VALLEY

RED RIVER VALLEY

YANKEE DOODLE

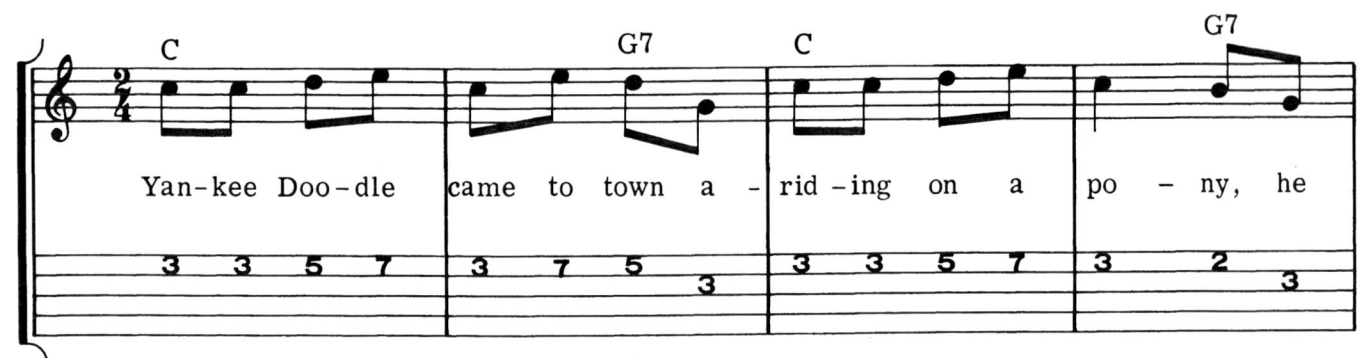
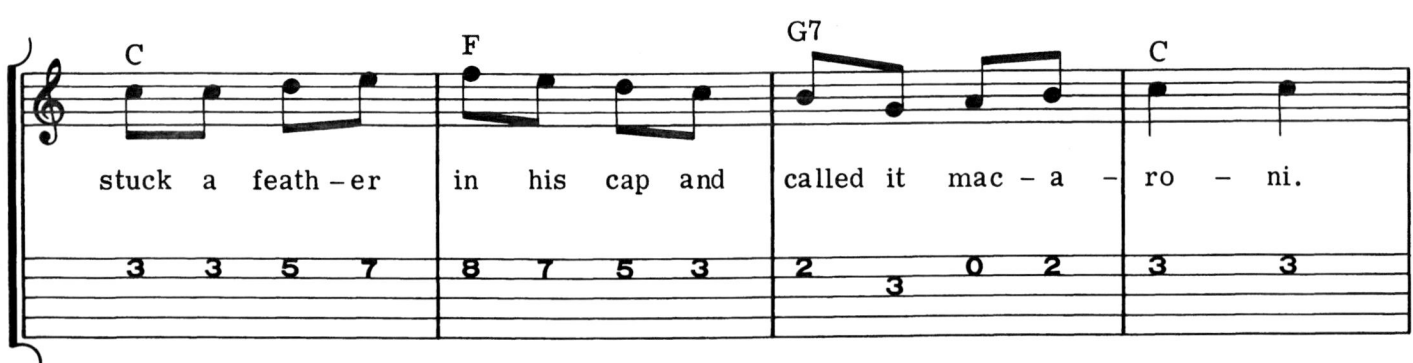
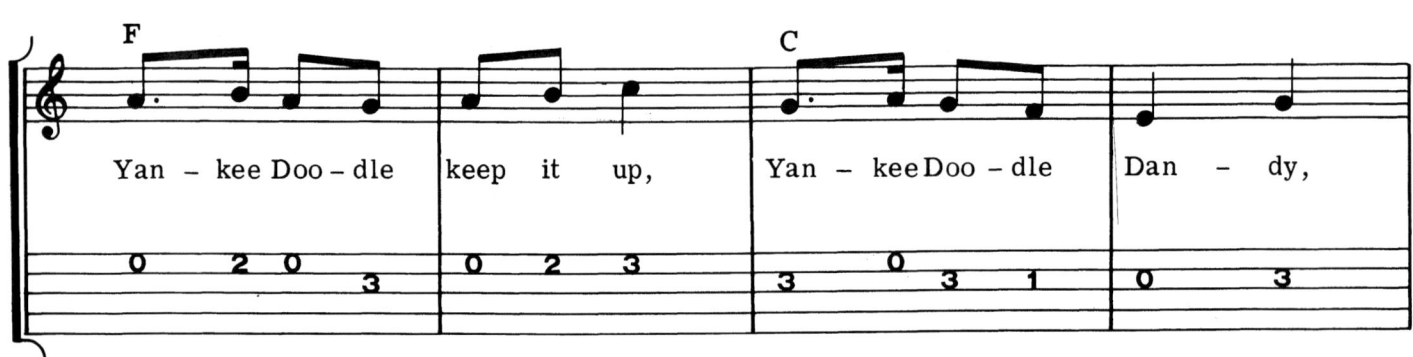

YANKEE DOODLE

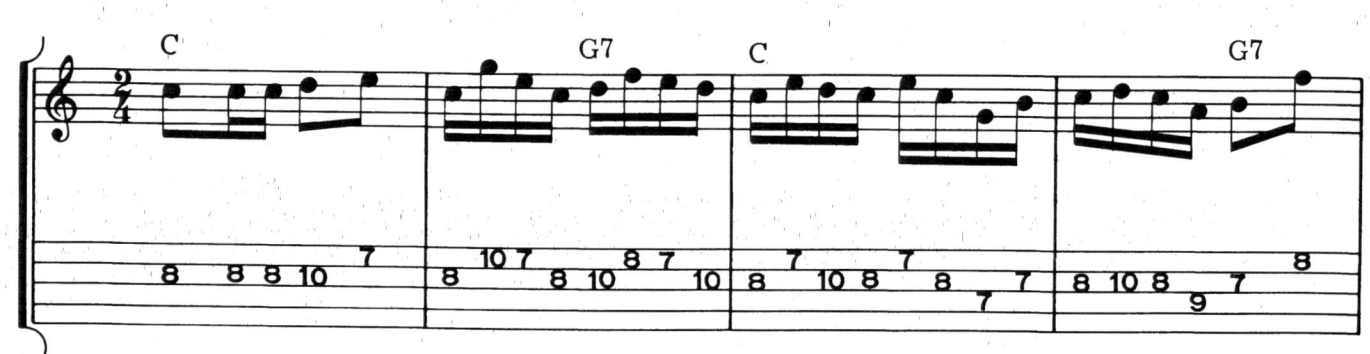
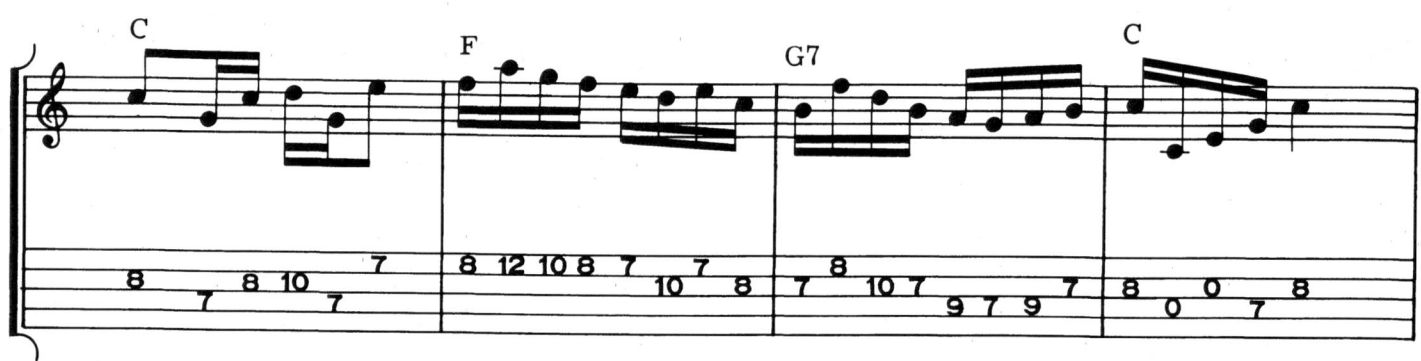
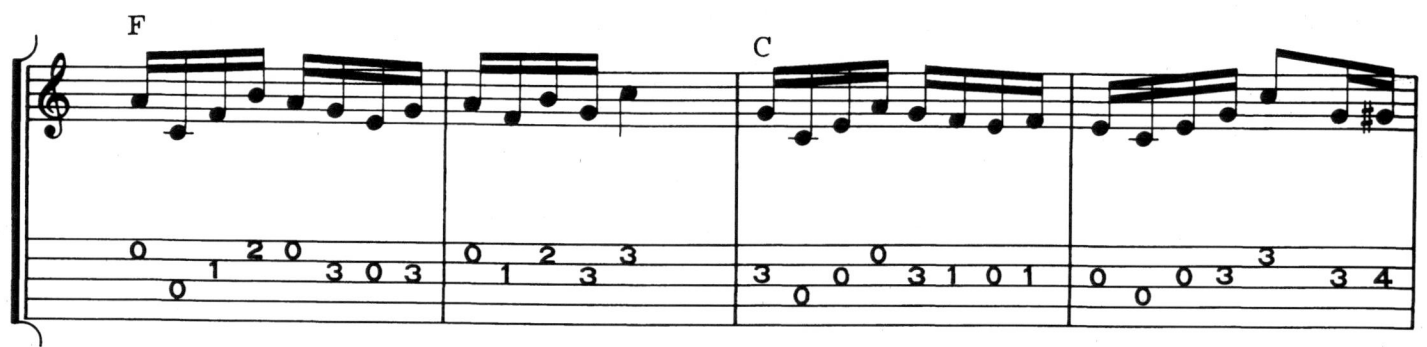

ALOHA OE

ALOHA OE

JOHNNY HAS GONE FOR A SOLDIER

3. I'll sell my flax, I'll sell my reel,
   Buy my love a sword of steel,
   So it in battle he may wield,
   Johnny has gone for a soldier.

JOHNNY HAS GONE FOR A SOLDIER

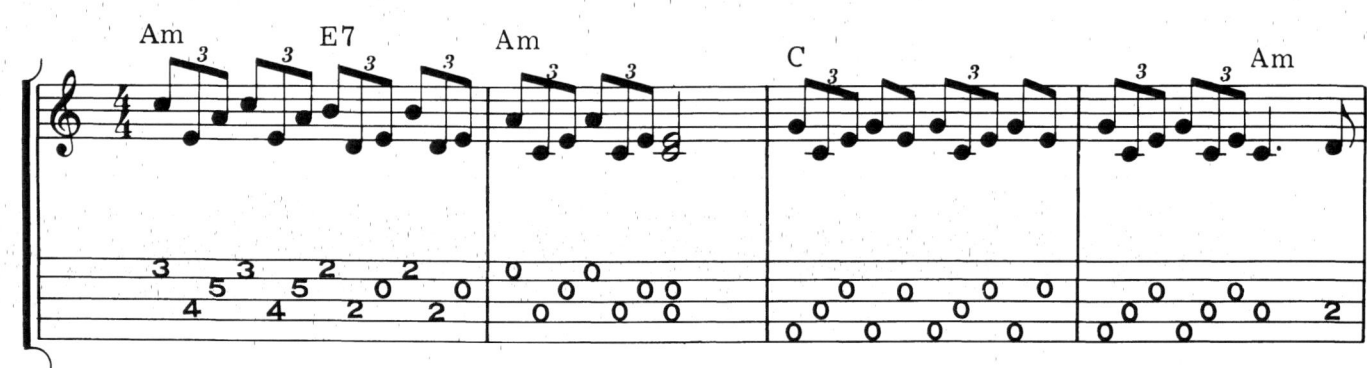
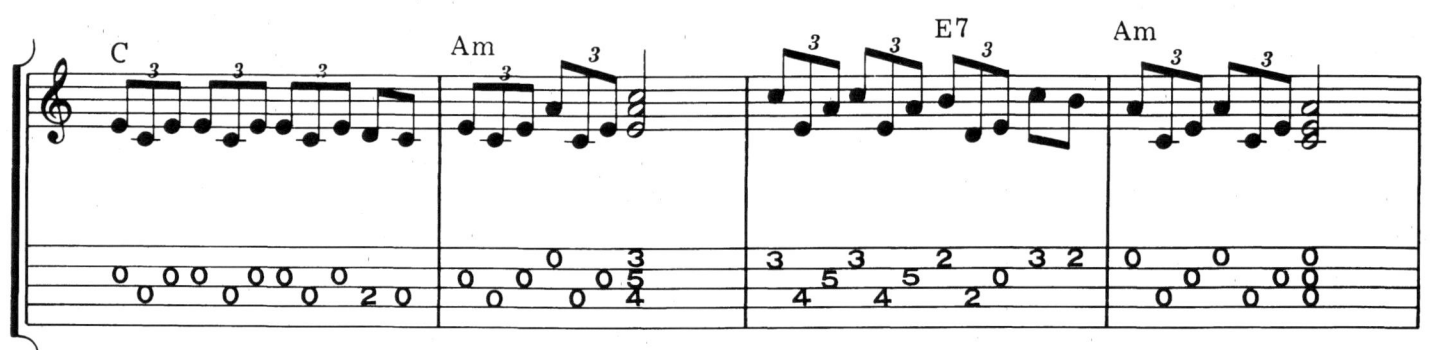
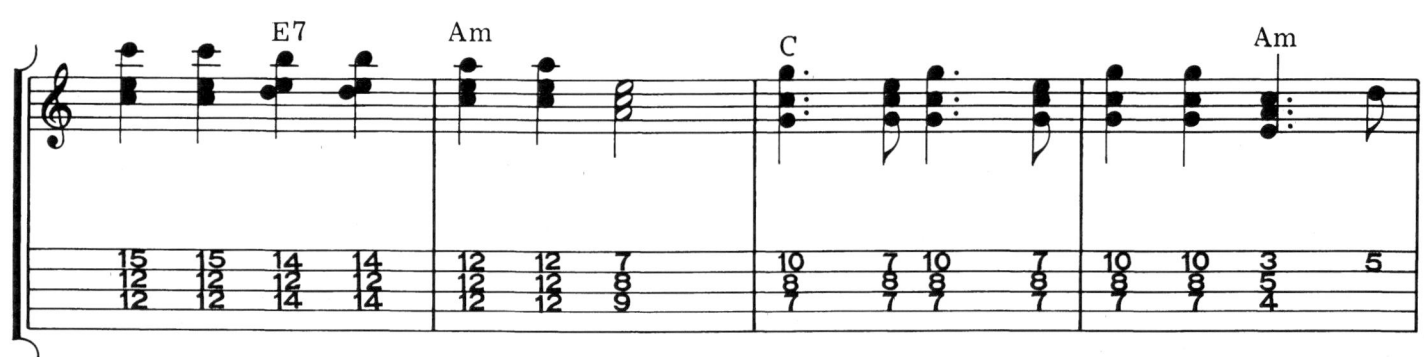

GOOBER PEAS

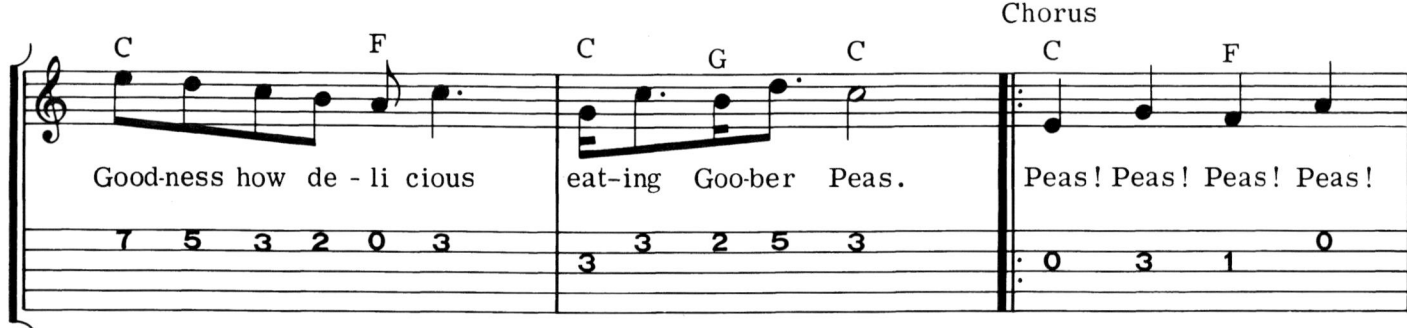
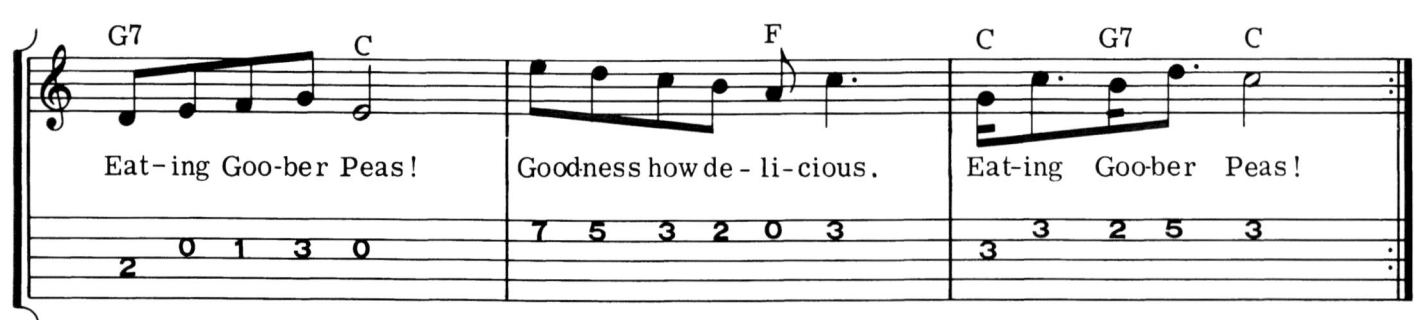

Just before the battle the general hears a row,
He says, "The Yanks are coming, I hear their rifles now,"
He turns around in wonder and what do you think he sees?
The Georgia Militia, eating Goober Peas! CHORUS

I think my song has lasted almost long enough.
The subject's interesting, but rhymes are mighty rough.
I wish this war was over, when free from rags and fleas,
We'd kiss our wives and sweethearts and gobble Goober Peas! CHORUS

GOOBER PEAS

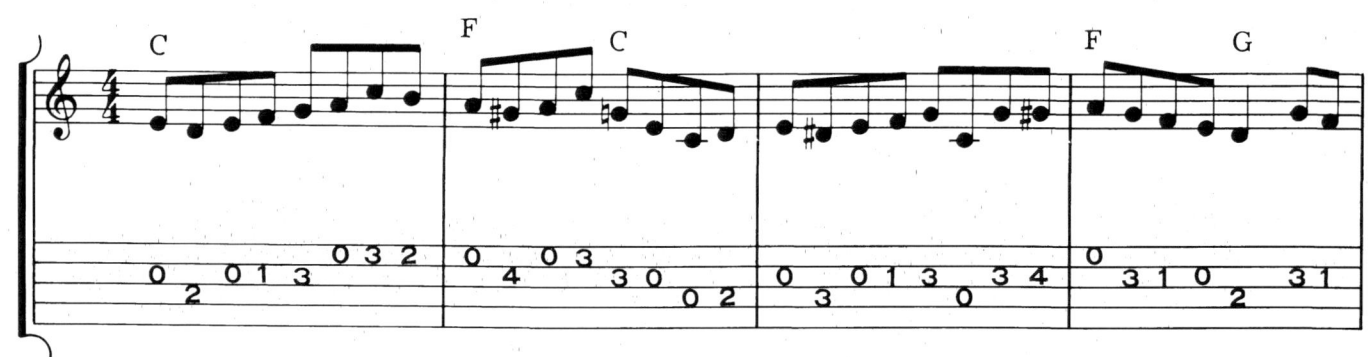
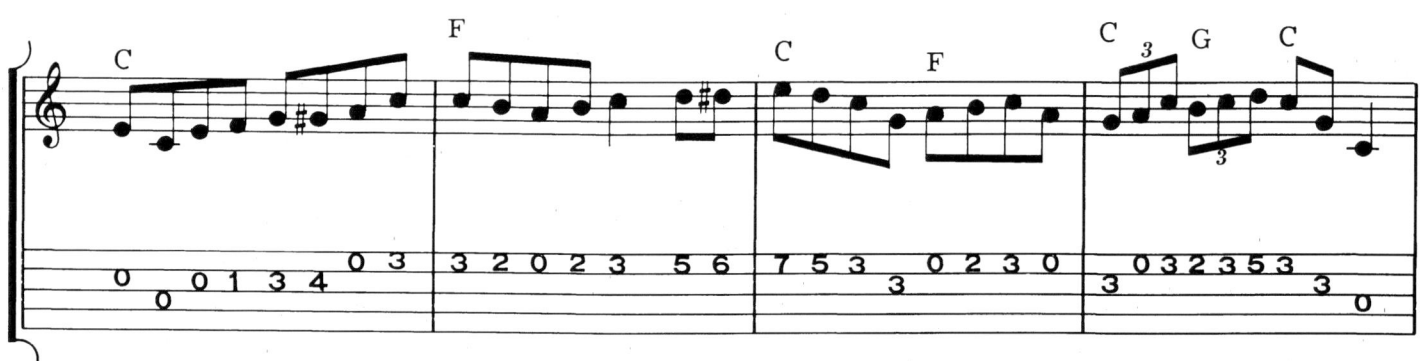
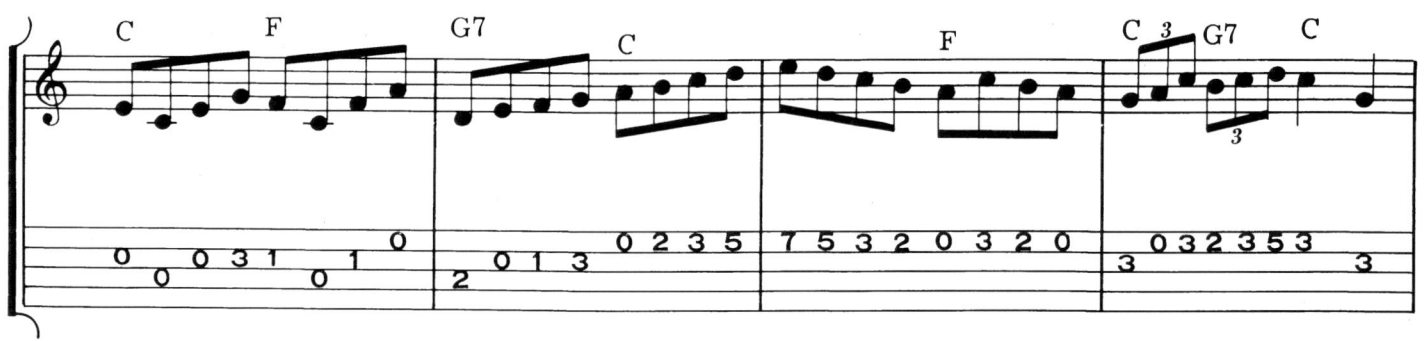
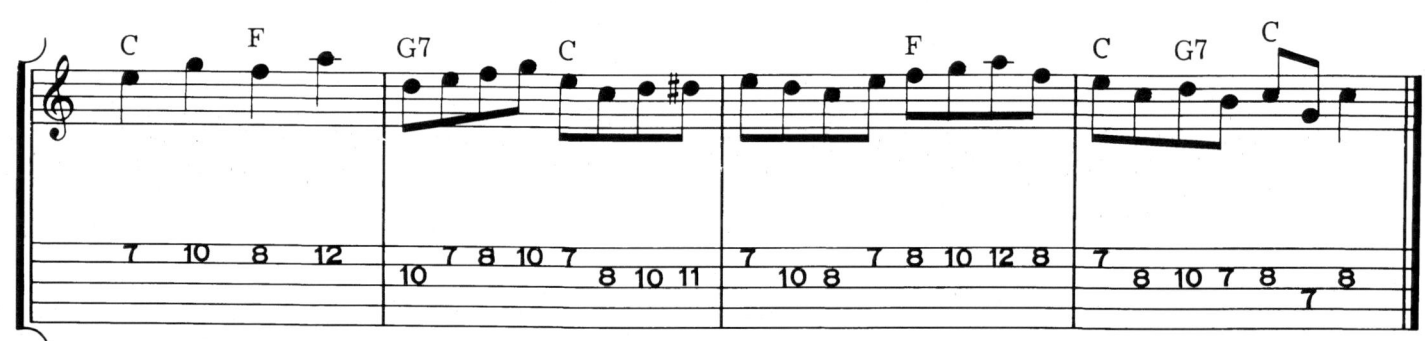

A-ROVING

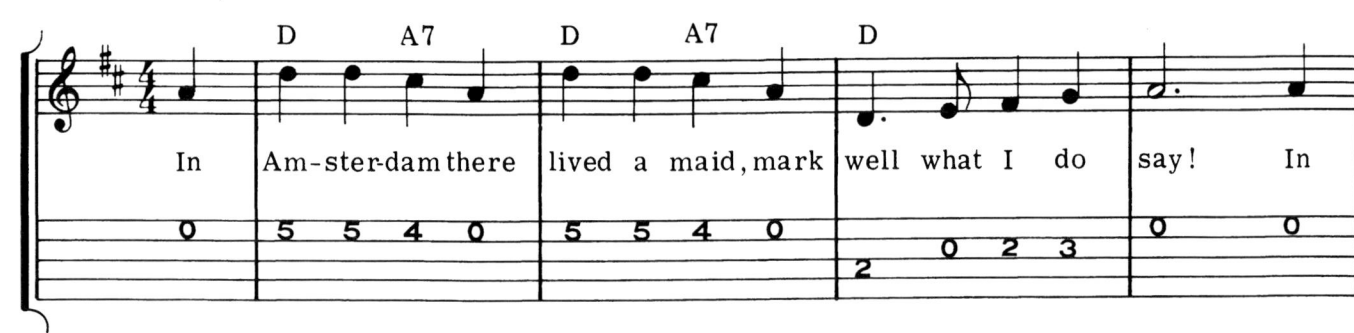
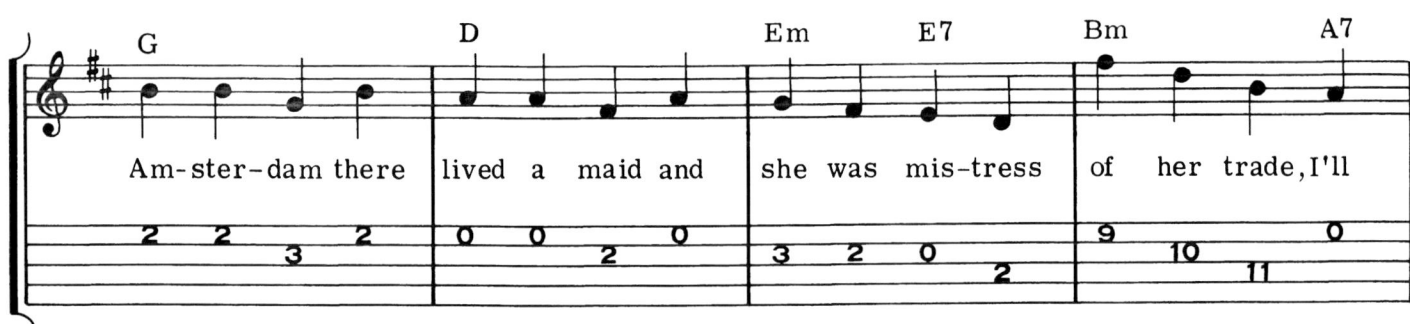
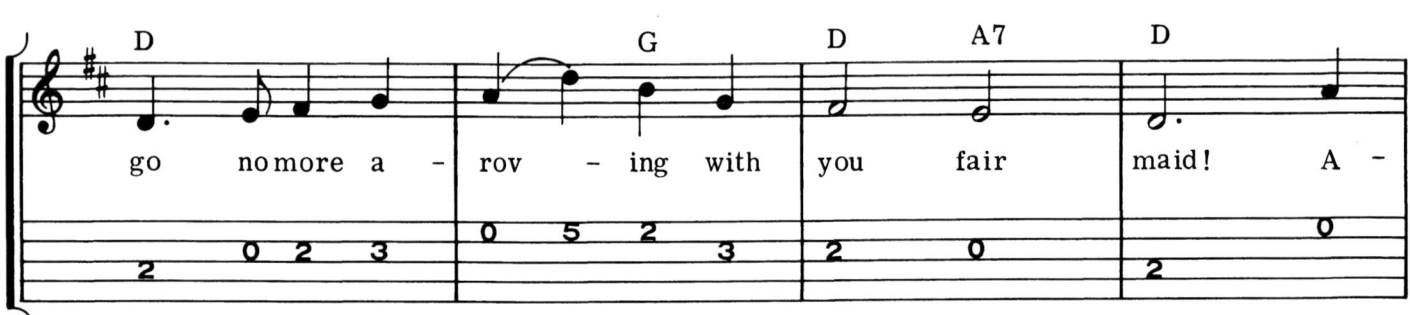
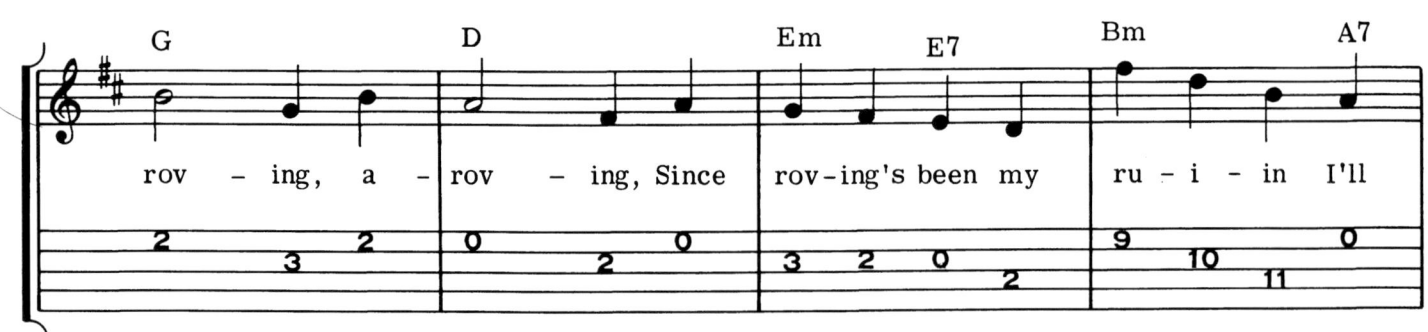
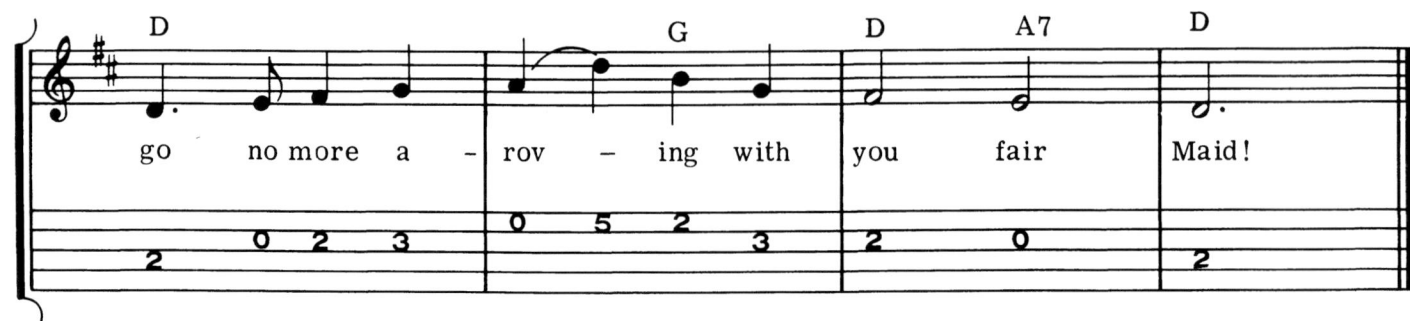

A-ROVING

CHISHOLM TRAIL

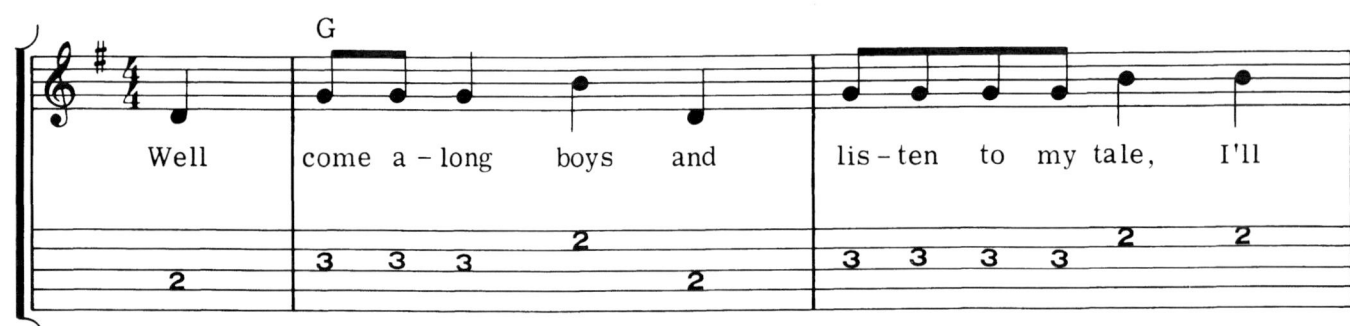

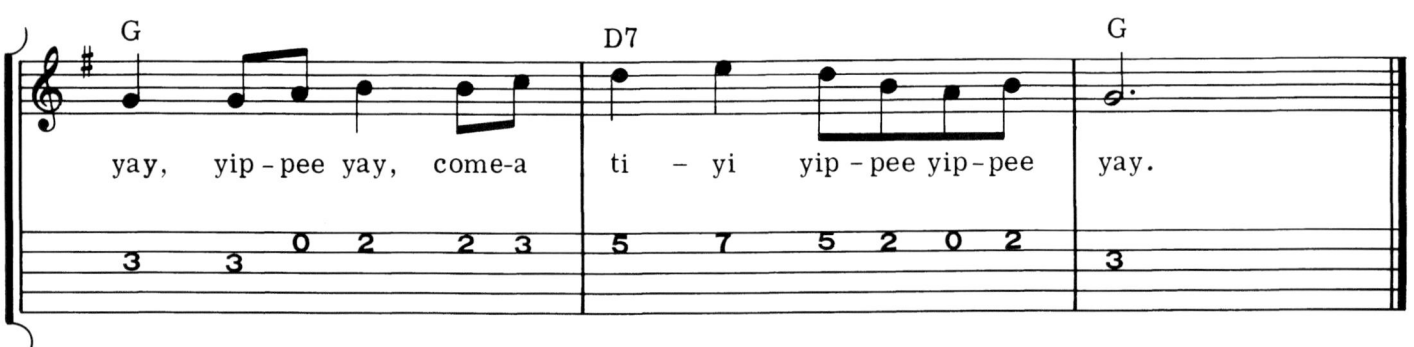

I started up the trail October twenty-third,
I started up the trail with the two-U herd,
Come-a ti yi yippee yippee yay, yippee yay,
Come a ti yi yippee yippee yay.

No chaps, no slicker and it's pourin' down rain,
I swear by gosh I'll never night herd again.
Come-a ti yi yippee yippee yay, yippee yay,
Come-a ti yi yippee yippee yay.

CHISHOLM TRAIL

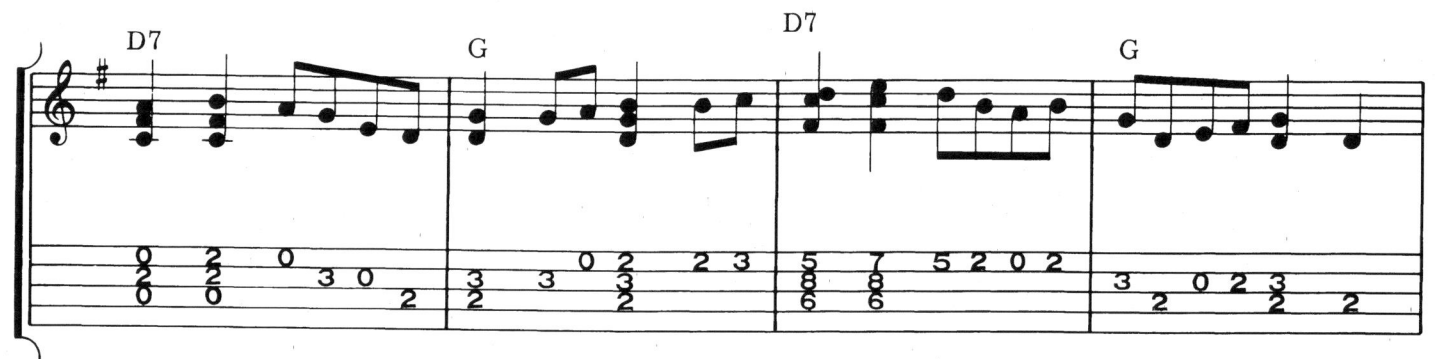

DEEP RIVER

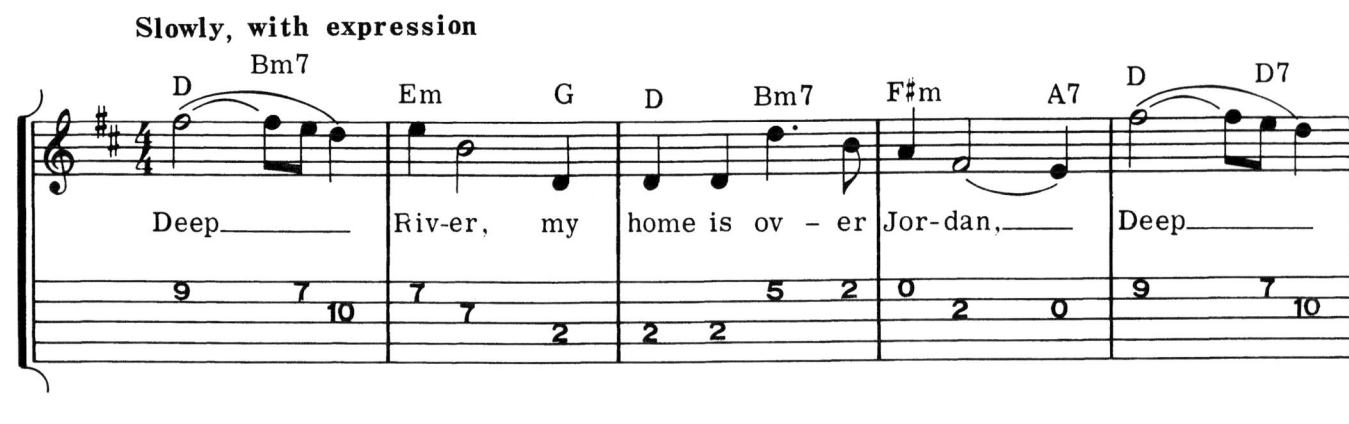
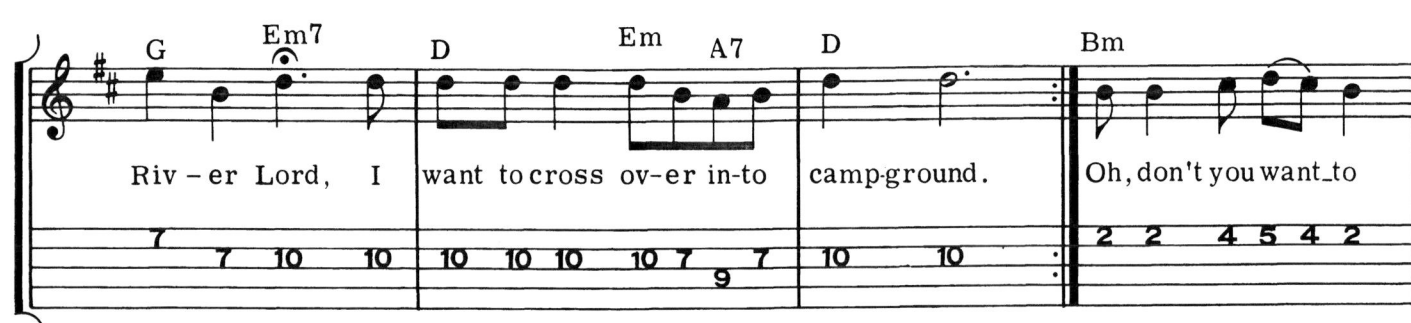
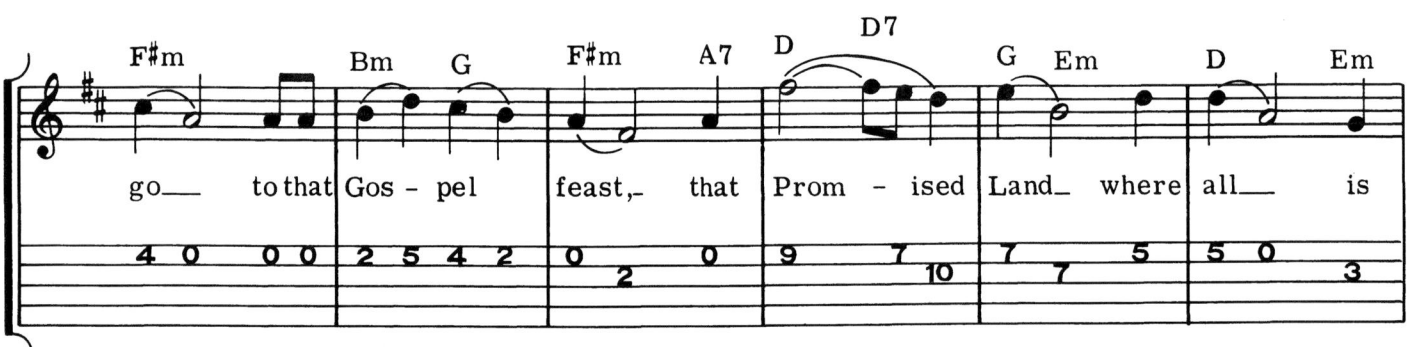
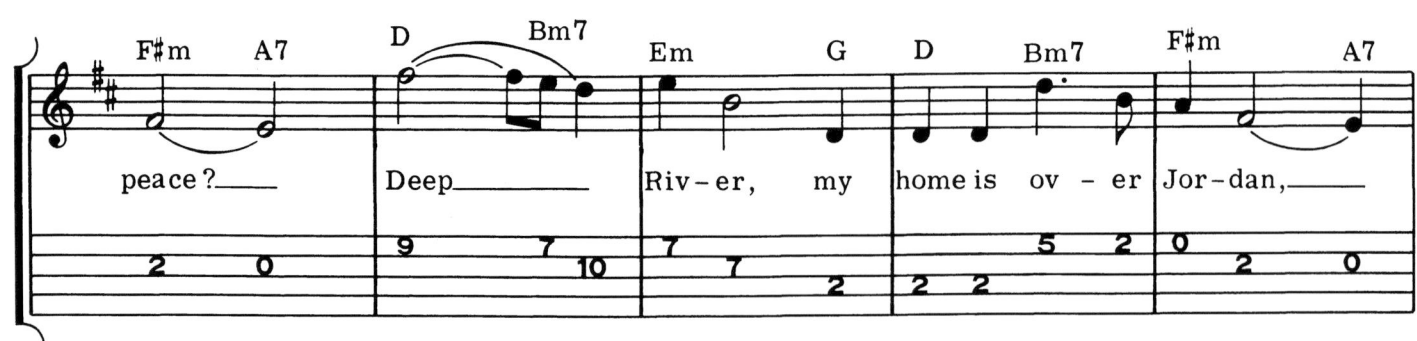

DEEP RIVER

BASIC CHORDS

Bb 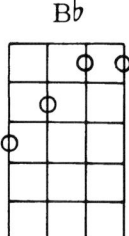   F 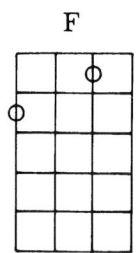   C 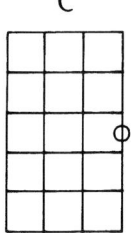   G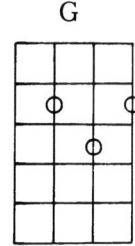

D 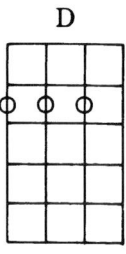   DM7 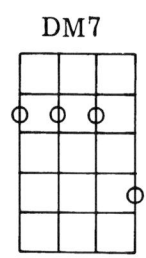   C7 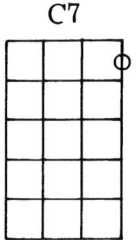   G7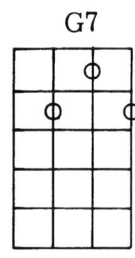

D7 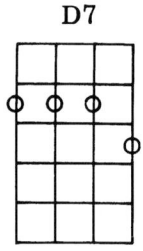   A7 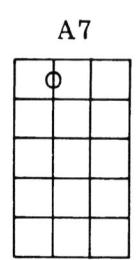   E7 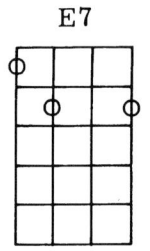   Fm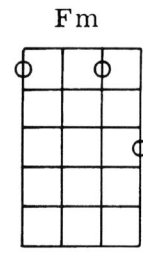

Gm 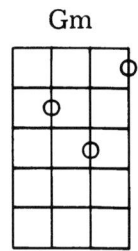   Dm 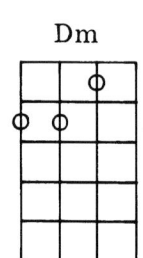   Am 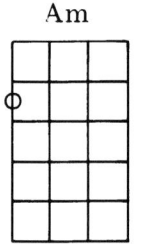   Em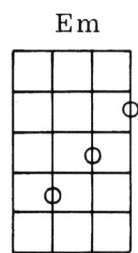

Bm 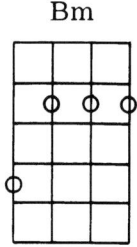   F#m 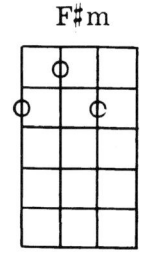   Bm7 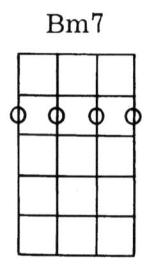   Em7 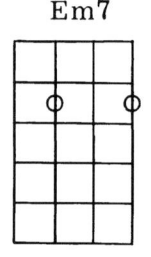   D+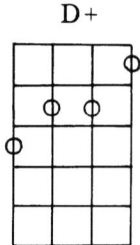

NOTES ON THE FINGERBOARD

The notes on the four strings of the ukulele are as follows:

1st string

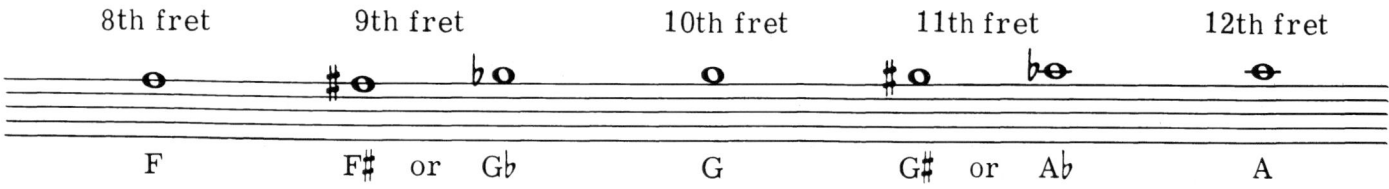

still 1st string

2nd string

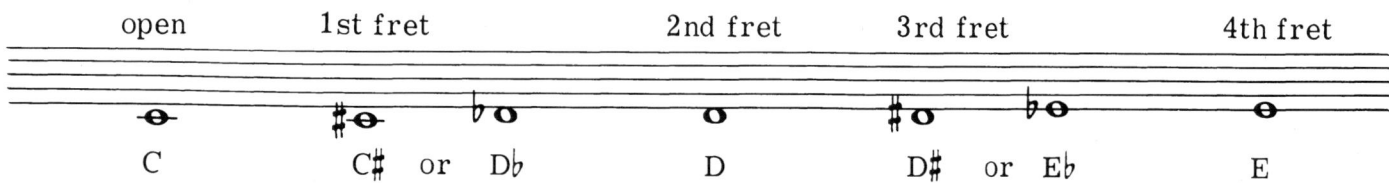

3rd string

Low G 4th string

High G 4th string is not used in playing melody notes.

SCALES

Scales are the basis for relating notes to each other in music. Most players use scales in their playing. The following exercise will help you play major scales in all keys and will help familiarize you with the fretboard.

SCALE EXERCISE

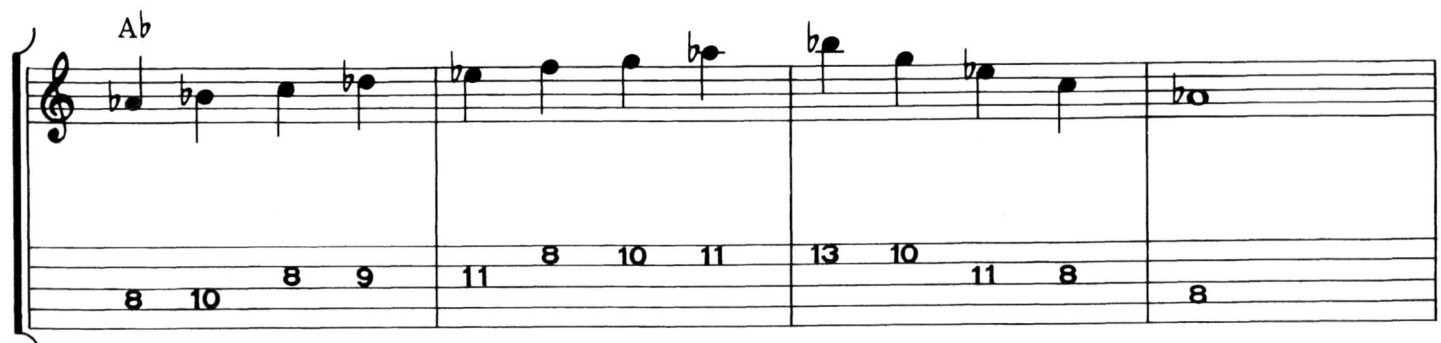
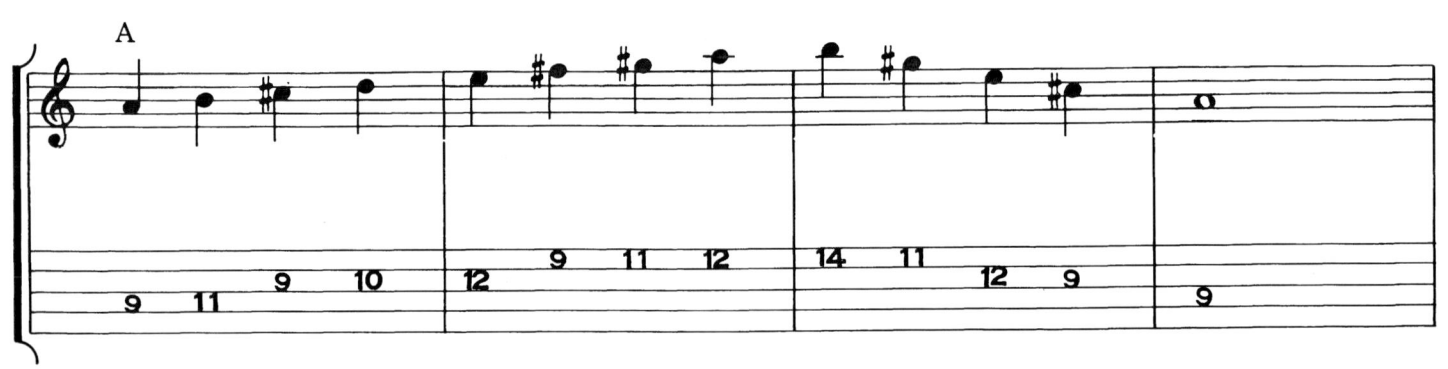
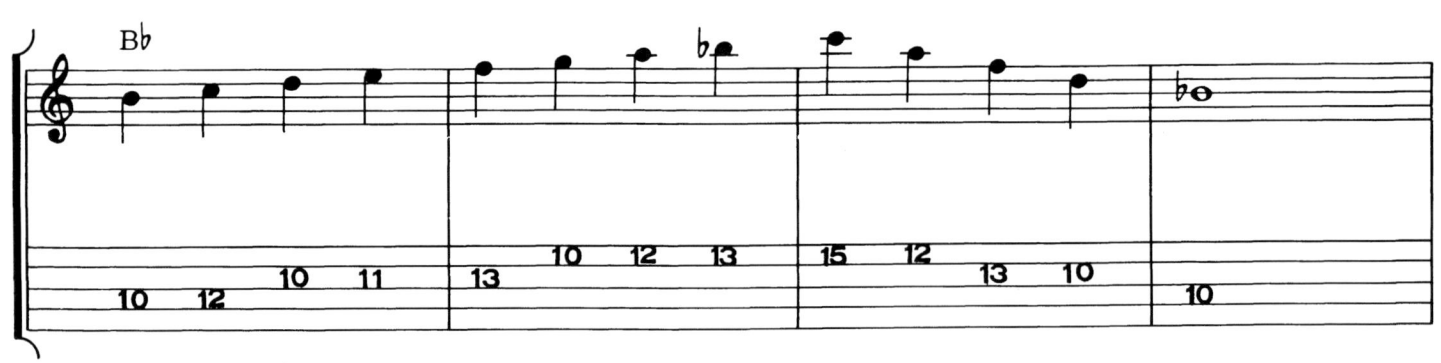
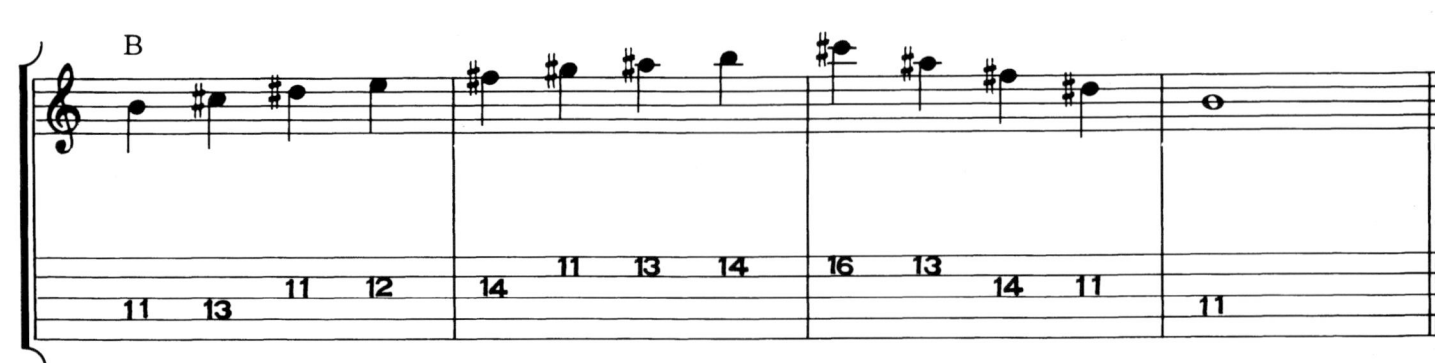